In *Leap of Faith*, my friend Ellie Lofaro r̲ ... Christians to place their trust solely in God through the cross of Jesus Christ.

Charles W. Colson, Chairman, Prison Fellowship Ministries

Ellie Lofaro is refreshing. She is passionate, clear thinking, and compassionate. From her wealth of experience and biblical knowledge, Ellie has given us a powerful encouragement to "trust God!" no matter what, no matter when, no matter where. Ellie is a mom with three kids and a husband, who invites you into her heart and allows you to live, laugh, and learn with her".

Jan Silvious, Speaker and author of *Big Girls Don't Whine*

Leap of Faith is filled with biblical truth, poignant personal stories, bottom-line honesty, and profound take-home value. With her characteristic humor woven through every chapter, Ellie Lofaro teaches us how to survive in a fallen world. Whether on the platform as a speaker, or as a writer of substance, Ellie is one of the finest communicators of our time.

Carol Kent, Author and President of *Speak Up!* Speaker Services

Ellie's latest offering, *Leap of Faith*, is her best work to date. You will be challenged, encouraged, inspired, and warmed by her fresh perspective and very practical application of timeless truths. The book reflects Ellie's direct, humorous, yet tender approach to life. I loved reading Leap of Faith-so will you.

Kathy Troccoli, Singer, speaker, and author of *Living in Love with Jesus*

With the color and vibrancy of a true Italian, Ellie Lofaro transports us to her childhood, where meals were "love affairs," and the family lingered long, reluctant to part. Then she transports us to the world of a personal God, to the greatest "love affair." You will want to linger long at this table, for it is a feast for the heart. I highly recommend *Leap of Faith*.

Dee Brestin, Teacher and author of *A Woman's Journey Through Psalms* and *Living in Love with Jesus*

To inquire about Ellie's speaking or writing ministry, please contact:

HEART, MIND & SOUL MINISTRIES
Ellie Lofaro
PO Box 9292
Reston, VA 20195
Phone/Fax 703.435.5334
Website: www.ellielofaro.com
E-Mail: ellie@ellielofaro.com

Other books by Ellie Lofaro available at your local Christian bookstore:

Slices of Life

ISBN:0-78143-743-1

Sitting down with this book is like chatting on the phone with a friend who trusts you enough to tell you what she really thinks. And what does Ellie think? From blond women to bumper stickers, bonbons to lice, God is precisely where we are so sure He cannot be. He is in our midst—in the ordinary events of our lives. "I LOVE THIS BOOK!"

—**Barbara Johnson**, Best-selling author and speaker

Bonding with the Blonde Women

ISBN: 0-78143-993-0

You can read these stories in bite-sized pieces, but you'll probably want to devour them all in one sitting! "Attenzione! My Italian friend is back. And, she's brought with her a batch of new, poignant stories ... full of thought and humor and charm. Do yourself a yourself a favor—read this book and enjoy it with a cup of espresso and biscotti. You'll be glad you did. Brava, Ellie."

—**Luci Swindoll**, Women of Faith speaker and author

LEAP OF FAITH

LEAP OF FAITH

EMBRACING THE LIFE
GOD PROMISED YOU

ELLIE LOFARO

Building the New Generation of Believers

An Imprint of Cook Communications Ministries
COLORADO SPRINGS, COLORADO • PARIS, ONTARIO
KINGSWAY COMMUNICATIONS, LTD., EASTBOURNE, ENGLAND

NexGen® is an imprint of
Cook Communications Ministries, Colorado Springs, CO 80918
Cook Communications, Paris, Ontario
Kingsway Communications, Eastbourne, England

LEAP OF FAITH

Cover Photo: Ken Rada Photography

First Printing, 2004
Printed in the United States of America
2 3 4 5 6 7 9 10 Printing/Year 08 07 06 05 04

Library of Congress Cataloging-in-Publication Data

Lofaro, Ellie.
    Leap of faith : embracing the life God promised you/ Ellie Lofaro.
    p. cm.
    Includes bibliographical references (p. 251).
    ISBN 0-7814-4070-X (pbk.)
    1. Christian women--Religious life.   I. Title.
BV4527.L635 2004
248.8'43--dc22

                                                2003027114

*I lovingly dedicate this book to three **incredible** kids who sacrificed the summer of 2003 in order for this project to come to fruition.*

Paris, Jordan and Capri—you're the stars in my sky. I'm eternally grateful God arranged for me to be your Mom. Thank you for being selfless as I answer His call.

CONTENTS

ACKNOWLEDGMENTS

My heart felt thanks to ...

My *devoted* husband **Frank**—Thank you for 22 years of safety, shelter and unconditional love. These are what every woman longs for. The road is long but it will always lead me back home to you.

My *wonderful* children **Paris, Jordan,** and **Capri**—Thank you for allowing me to practice my mothering skills on you (Sorry about the cooking).

My *beloved* buddy **Kathy Troccoli**—Mount Rushmore has cracks but you choose to see the beauty. You are a gift. Your review of this manuscript was invaluable.

My *mighty* mentor **Patsy Clairmont**—They may refer to you as being "little," but as I've gotten closer, all I see is a giant. Thank you for helping me grow.

My *favorite* teachers **Jan Silvious, Dee Brestin, Carol Kent,** and **Beth Moore**—Your passion for the Word ignites mine. Thank you for bearing a standard.

My *precious* **Prayer Partners**—May God repay you a hundred fold for the labor of love we call "intercession." Thank you for "covering me" as I go and tell.

Pastor Donnell Jones—Your *inspired* sermon on Genesis 12 fanned a flame.

The Bright Pond Bible Study—You are my reality check. I *love* being together.

Shari Connealy, president of Maggpie Communications Inc. and also a *generous* neighbor—Thank you for a top notch, classy website.

Susan Tjaden, My *gifted* editor—You brought *my* new book and *your* new baby into the world at the same time. I'm impressed. You're tired. Put those feet up!

Cook Communications Ministries—In the words of CCM president David Mehlis; "The *best* is yet to come." I'm honored to be part of the vision.

Mary Ann Lackland of Fluency—For *excellent* creative direction.

Lord Jesus—You continue to pour out deep joy along the journey. I am abundantly blessed and I understand why "much is required." *How I need you.*

The leap of faith is not
over a canyon
or into a fire.
It does not necessitate
a mindless transference
of my logic or my trust
into the unknown.

This leap of faith is
into the strong arms
of a loving God.

There is no safer place.

I am a Christian. I believe with all my heart, mind, and soul that Jesus Christ came to earth to save and secure the future of the human race. I believe His teachings were accurately recorded in the Gospels, and that His story is told from Genesis to Revelation. The Bible is my manual for living. God made me, so when I need to be tuned up, hooked up, or lifted up—I return to the Maker of my soul. He knows me fully and loves me completely. He has a plan for my life but offers me free will to choose as I please. He sent His only Son to pay my spiritual debt and has personally promised that I will live forever. My God is remarkable.

I am a suburban housewife. The wife of Frank, the mother of Paris, Jordan, and Capri, and the guardian of the dog Bella. I'm behind on the laundry. I'm late for the car pool. I'm out of milk. The "to do" list is not getting shorter, and I see no hope of that happening in the next twenty years. The guilt that comes with never conquering the "to do" list is getting bigger. The awareness of time slipping away is growing keener. The offers for health, wealth, and happiness have become more frequent. The ominous headlines hang over my "safe" nest like foreboding clouds and angry lightning. That's reality.

This is a book about faith. So just what does the Old Testament, written thousands of years ago, have to do with *my* busy life? Despite the craziness and busyness of life—in the face of piles of dirty laundry and empty milk cartons—I have made some meaningful observations in the thirty-something years of my faith journey. God has asked me to believe His promises—and I do. He has told me that I can be an "overcomer"—and I am. He desires for me to leave a legacy—and with His help, I will. It's really that simple. Like most people, I am intimidated by heady spiritual teachings and lofty academic treatises. I am not a scholar nor a theologian nor even a great writer, but I *can* attest to the faithfulness of God. So can you. God calls me to climb higher, dig deeper, and stretch further. And in spite of my good intentions, I often fall along the way. Even so, I'm thankful that He catches me. I've experienced heartache, sorrow, and bruised knees. But I continue to take leaps of faith into the arms of the One who holds my future and helps me to stand through every trial. I trust God because He is trustworthy. And as you read these pages, I pray that you will be inspired and encouraged to take your own leap of faith. God is kind and generous to reveal Himself to anyone who seeks Him … even a suburban housewife.

PART ONE

CHAPTER ONE

CAPITAL "C" CHRISTIAN

SUNDAYS IN BROOKLYN

I grew up in a nice family in New York, the second of five children. Dad was born in Brooklyn and Mom was born in Milan, Italy. My father provided well for us and life was good. He was the ninth of eleven children, born to Italian immigrants who came to Ellis Island to pursue the American dream. Family gatherings, which commenced every Sunday afternoon at 1:00, were loud, emotive, and intimidating to anyone outside the family. Come to think of it, there were no outsiders, except for an occasional date accompanying one of my cousins. By the time we all married, there were thirty-four first cousins in all.

The Sabbath was sacred at my paternal grandparents', Papa and Mama Mannarino's, house—but not for reasons one might guess. Their grown children would never think of being late for the traditional macaroni and gravy. (They *never* called it pasta and sauce.) There is an Italian saying; *"Al tavolo, non sei vecchio."* ("At the table, we don't grow old.") For Italians, food is more than a meal. It is an occasion, a feast, a love affair. The table was a microcosm of the culture and a visual study of the hierarchy—in this case, of the patriarch, Giuseppe. The table was where everyone made eye contact. Arguments that may have started at the dinner table ended when Giuseppe raised his open hand and said *"Basta!"* ("Enough!").

We sat in two shifts; the kids ate first and then the adults. The adults would then sit for hours as the meal progressed from the antipasto, to the macaroni, to the gravy-drenched meatballs and sausage, to the veal cutlets, mashed potatoes, artichokes and salad, to the fruit and nuts, and eventually to the desserts. Yes, there were *many* desserts. Everybody stopped at their favorite local bakery on Sunday morning before heading over. We children sporadically returned from the TV room and the front stoop to seek out adult laps where we received a hug, a pinch, and a taste of whatever they were having.

Communication with the grandchildren was fairly basic. We were given simple directives: "Go wash your hands! Go sit down! Go eat! Go upstairs! Go outside! Go kiss Grandma!" The only meaningful conversation took place at the table. I'm not referring to deep, spirited discussion of politics or religion. It was more along the lines of the price of tomatoes, which neighbor moved, what year Joey Donatelli died, and how the Yankees were doing. Characteristically, the decibel level in the room went from very loud to very, *very* loud.

Until my Confirmation ceremony, I was under the impression that God's last name started with a D. We never said grace, although Mom *did* insist that Father MacDonald sprinkle holy water into our brand-new swimming pool before any human body parts ever touched the deep end. There was an awareness of the *existence* of God—but not the *experience* of God. Religion came up from time to time, but there wasn't much discussion—other than ours was right and everyone else's was wrong.

ARE YOU A CHRISTIAN?

Nonetheless, I was a seeker, and at age fourteen I began my search for a relational God. It didn't take long to find Him. One day while serving as president of the Student Council at Candlewood Junior High, someone shattered my above average existence with one simple question: "Are you a Christian?"

I was a bit offended. "Am I Christian?" I was Italian—that made me a Christian, didn't it? "I'm a good person. I follow the Ten Commandments. I even go to church on all the important days. Of course I'm a Christian!"

Not satisfied with my glib answer, this friend said to me, "Well, Jesus said to forget the Ten Commandments. He said, 'There are just two. You have to love God with all your heart, mind, and soul, and then love other people like yourself.' If you're doing those two, everything else falls into place. So, do you love God with all your heart, mind, and soul, Ellie?"

Even at that young age, I knew the answer. I didn't love Jesus like that. I didn't even know it was possible. I didn't know He loved me and died for me. I was stunned when my friend explained how Jesus suffered and died on the cross for my sins. *My* sins?

GO AND TELL

When I asked Jesus to reside in my heart and be my constant companion, I began a relationship with the living God. I have been amazed by His goodness and love ever since. I am fully convinced of His existence and committed to the Great Commission to "go and tell." After all, when you fall in love—you tell people. When you get married—you tell people. When you have a baby—you tell people. And when you find out there's a way to live in Paradise forever and ever … well, you just don't keep that kind of thing to yourself.

As I grew older, a little wiser, and closer to the Lord, I began to realize why so many people declare their faith to be 'personal'. It's often said that many people have placed God in a box. He is compartmentalized. He is too big and too vague and too scary. Some have their own custom version of God, while others are so angry that they "can't even go there." The topic of knowing God personally was a big no-no with family and certain friends. Heads would shake, eyes would roll, and the hushed response was, "It's personal. Some things are not meant for discussion." Could it be that for some, there's not *much* to discuss?

THE CAPITAL "C" CHRISTIAN

The term, "Christian," is used so loosely in today's world. When I married Frank, my sweet Nona asked if he was a "Christian boy." She was not asking, "Does he love Jesus? Will he be the spiritual leader of your home?" No, what she meant was something altogether different.

The most recent Gallup Poll says that 80 percent of America is "Christian."[1] Maybe you had the same response to that news as I did. *Really?* Sitting in a pew doesn't make us Christians any more than being in a bakery makes us baguettes!

Many of us are born into a religion. I respect religion and acknowledge a person's right to choose one or none. Religion has an important place in the world, but what is religion without relationship? Jesus spoke at length about the horrors of religiosity void of true devotion.

And what about the part where we are supposed to love God with all our heart, mind, and soul? In early 2003, America watched the war in Iraq unfold on live television. Every morning in the 100-degree days marked by sand, sweat, and bugs, coalition soldiers reported for duty and awaited their orders. Over the years, I have developed a profile of what I call a Capital "C" Christian. A Capital "C" Christian simply wakes up in the morning and says to God, "Reporting for duty, Sir." Capital "C" Christians know why they're here and where they're going. They know the joy of going through life *and* through death straight into an everlasting life.

You are a Capital "C" Christian when you love Jesus Christ with all of your being. I am glad to declare that I am a Capital "C" Christian. Highly flawed, fully forgiven, and greatly favored. I count my resume, my repertoire, and my real estate as loss compared to the glory of God's provisions. I do not have a death wish, but neither do I fear death. I am saved.

DWINDLING HEAT

When I first became a Christian, I didn't walk to Bible study—I ran. I couldn't wait for prayer meetings to start. I was excited about being part of a Christian coffeehouse that met in a basement every Friday night. No air conditioning and no ventilation. Yet over a hundred people showed up to sit in folding chairs and listen as guitars strummed uplifting melodies. Everybody looked beautiful and smelled nice.

However, somewhere along the way I lost some of my childlike enthusiasm, and I gained a critic's eye. If I went to that coffeehouse today, I'm sure I would notice body odors (mine and theirs). I'd be bothered that there were never enough chairs. I would cast a dubious eye on those who look different. Maybe my heart has grown a bit cold.

Where is that childlike faith and "first love" enthusiasm? What happened? For so many, Christianity has become a mediocre meander along the lazy river of life. At times, our faith can seem feeble and anemic—our Christian pulse barely detectable. Satisfied to have taken the initial step, we're now just incubating in a warm nest.

THE LEAP OF FAITH

Just about the time our friends and family get used to the idea that we might possibly be "religious," a challenge to our faith comes along. It may be an illness. An accident. An over-whelming financial problem or family crisis. Something unexpected and most often uninvited drives us to the cross-roads of commitment—a point where we must believe *all*

Jesus said or muddle through and wind up disillusioned and disaffected on the other side. It's a gutsy move to go from the known to the unknown. Beyond the tried and proven there is something else: a leap of faith from a marginal existence to radical, kingdom-minded living.

We are continually challenged to climb the ladder of faith to the toe-curling edge of a platform representing all we have experienced thus far—all we have known about God versus all we have yet to experience regarding who He is. Is it a blind leap into the unknown, as the Danish philosopher Kierkegaard once proposed? Certainly *not*. In fact, the leap of faith is an eyes-wide-open experience. There is much to know about the God waiting for us with open arms. And He welcomes the questions. He invites the seeker. As Francis Schaeffer commented, "He is there and He is not silent."[2] This leap of faith is not over a canyon or into a fire. It does not necessitate a mindless transference of my logic or my trust into the unknown. This leap of faith is into the strong arms of a loving God. There is no safer place.

Thomas Aquinas, a theologian, philosopher, and apologist of the medieval church, said, "Faith uses reason and reason cannot succeed in finding truth without faith. Reason accompanies but does not *cause* faith."[3] Faith and reason are knit together. It's difficult to have faith at the funeral of a two year old. It's tough to consider God's goodness even as a spouse walks out the door forever. The rebellious child. The baby with spina bifida. Apart from faith, it would be impossible in the midst of many of life's circumstances to step back, look at the big picture and say, "Even so, God is good." The leap of faith is about sticking it out and stepping up with all our might to believe and accept all God offers us.

I have come to appreciate the adage, "The more I know, the more I don't know." As a twenty-five-year-old Christian, I was sure I had all the answers including why bad things happen to good people. I had found the truth, so I "needed" to be able to defend the truth. Sometimes, as young believers, we want to have all the answers. It would make things so much simpler. Now, over thirty years have passed since those early days and although I consider myself wiser, I know I don't have all the answers. I don't understand why bad things happen. I don't understand why life can be so hard. I don't understand holocausts and famine and slavery. I'll never understand fourteen-year-old suicide bombers, or why death comes to some so early, so cruelly, so suddenly.

The underlying assumption is that once we become Christians, we will have a happy life. *Hakuna matada!* That's *Swahili* for "no worries." The truth is that as Christians, we are to take up our cross—and our sadness and suffering—and follow Him. There *will* be trouble; Jesus told us so. That's why the Bible talks about "the fellowship of sharing in his sufferings" (Phil. 3:10). Our response to the inevitable adversity of life reveals to the world what we believe about His promises. I have no idea why there is pain, but I do know there's a God who has made extraordinary promises to love us, care for us, and protect us. He will make us more like Him. He will redeem us. He is the keeper of *every* promise. Christians are not immune to trouble, but we are empowered to respond differently than those without relationship with the Savior.

When our daughter Paris was three years old, she joined Frank and me on a business trip to Phoenix. Frank went off to meetings. Paris and I went to the hotel pool. It was a leisurely afternoon, and after two carefree hours my lifeguard radar was no longer fully engaged. Paris walked deeper into the middle of the pool not realizing a gradual decline in the grade. As I chatted with another conventioneer's wife, I turned to see a little hand grasping just above the water. By the time I got to her, she was dazed, turning blue, and semi-conscious. I prayed and called out God's name in the midst of chaos.

Fast forward to the emergency room of the Phoenix Children's Hospital. The life-saving procedures were painful for a mother's heart to endure but welcomed nonetheless. Paris was admitted into the children's ward for 24-hour observation. Snuggled against my baby girl in her hospital bed, I felt relieved when she finally fell asleep—although I stayed awake most of the night. As I looked around, it became apparent that some of the other children were not going home. I struggled to hold back my tears.

Paris was released the next morning, but my thoughts were held captive by what I saw the night before. I could have lost my daughter that day, but I didn't. Yet there are many heartbroken parents whose cries to God seem to have gone unheard. I have not lost a child or a spouse or a close friend to the grave. But I choose to believe that when such a painful day comes—and it will—I will cling to the promises of God. I have seen the peace that passes human understanding, and witnessed the leap of faith taken by those who love and follow Him.

GET READY TO FLY

So how do we go from nominal living to this extraordinary place of promise? Hocus-pocus? Three simple steps? First, we need to understand that the leap of faith is not *our* idea. Faith is God's idea. Aquinas explained it this way: "Faith is a gift of God and no one can believe without it. One must receive by faith those things that can be known by reason, as well as those things that lie above reason."[4] God loved us first, and we take that step because of His faithfulness to us (1 John 4:19). Scripture says, "Therefore, the promise comes by faith, so that it may be by grace" (Rom. 4:16). God gave us His promises so that during times of trouble we might flex our faith and stay afloat. It's how we go from a marginal existence to realizing we have great purpose.

It's a scary place—dangling somewhere between what has already been and all that could potentially be. I imagine some will find their palms sweating as they consider that next step. They're clenching the trapeze bar of security and familiarity, wondering if they're ready to let go at just the right moment and catch what God has in store for them. But it's precisely where we find the faith to believe all we have heard about Jesus and His promises to be true, real, and relevant. It's also where our faith in Christ bears out politically and ideologically despite the bombardment of "intellectual" data that speaks to the contrary. The leap of faith I'm talking about is *that* radical. So why should you be willing to take the leap? I thought you'd never ask.

TAKE THE LEAP

Ⅰt was a typical Sunday afternoon. We had all stripped off our church garb and changed into sweats and thick socks. The kids settled into a rented video, Frank was inhaling the *New York Times* and I was—you guessed it—doing laundry. As I carried load number four to the bedrooms, Frank peered above the paper.

"Ellie, did you know that in the back of the business section of every major city's newspaper is a list of names representing funds, corporations, endowments, lawsuit settlements, and distant uncles who have bequeathed money to unknowing recipients?"

As I smashed sloppily folded tablecloths into a kitchen drawer, he proceeded to expound upon the topic at hand. He explained that these lists represent a fortune in unclaimed funds. There are even online search sites and computer software programs to help reunite people with their unclaimed property. Scan the names and you'll see hundreds of people whose unclaimed money is being safeguarded by state officials. Billions of dollars go unclaimed every year.

How do these remarkable oversights happen? Forgotten safe deposit boxes, misplaced savings accounts, uncollected insurance policies, unreturned rent and utility deposits, credit balances, forgotten layaway deposits, uncashed checks, credit memos, refunds—the list goes on and on. I can see losing some spare change between the pillows on the sofa or washing a ten-dollar bill in your jeans pocket—but hundreds of thousands of dollars? If someone can prove he or she is entitled to the money, the state comptroller will gladly return it to that individual. The trick is getting people to respond to the ad. Most Americans don't bother even to search for this money.

I'm thinking about placing an ad of my own. An announcement to the untold thousands of Christians who have no idea they are sitting on a windfall. I believe it would read something like this:

Public Announcement

Fellow account owner wishes to reunite other shareholders with unclaimed funds of incalculable worth. Assets available to the holder of unclaimed property include eternal blessings, measureless joy, righteousness, fullness of power, security, and an imperishable inheritance. Claimant is justified, seen as perfect, beyond condemnation, and destined to enjoy rightful status as a partner with the account Guarantor, Jesus Christ.

Please note:

Earthly return of account Guarantor is imminent. After said return, all funds will be returned to Guarantor as unclaimed.

Do you think there would be any takers? We are children of a King. According to birthright, that makes us princes and princesses. Sadly, we often choose to live as if we're spiritual paupers. Right at this moment, no matter where life finds you this day, you have at your disposal a wealth of opportunity, blessing, and promise found in Christ. Yes, this wealth belongs to you! I'm not referring to any kind of "get rich quick" theology. I am referring to the abundant life that God offers.

MEMBERSHIP HAS ITS PRIVILEGES

In their successful campaign to attract credit card holders, American Express wooed the country with the luring promise that "Membership has its privileges." That was a highly successful campaign because since kindergarten, we have all wanted to belong, to fit in, and to enjoy the perks of the pack. And truth be told, we *all* love privileges.

Frank and I sign up for all of the reward programs we think will benefit us. We are loyal to certain hotel chains, airlines, and rental car companies and, in return, those organizations provide us with benefits. In today's vernacular, these benefits are referred to as "perks." Members have come to expect certain returns on their investments. Imagine our delight in taking the three kids to Europe a few summers ago and having all five roundtrip flights fully paid for by mileage points. Now, that's a perk! Frank stays on top of how many points are in our account when we book a room or fly a certain airline. We travel frequently, and we're very attentive when it comes to redeeming points. We read through all the fine print so we know what's coming to us. After all, we grew up in New York, where everybody loves a good bargain.

If you don't believe Christianity comes with privileges, consult your membership manual. Peruse a pocket Bible Promise Book so you can discover what you are entitled to as a child of the King. Are you aware of all the earthly and eternal benefits you can enjoy when you have Jesus living in your heart? Do you understand what that entails? Are you claiming your inheritance? Every promise God has given in His Word is for each one of us. The Bible tells us, "For no matter how many promises God has made, they are 'Yes' in Christ" (2 Cor. 1:20). The life you always wanted—the peace, the promises, the protection—it's all there in black and white (check out the red ink as well!) It's there for the asking. It's there for the taking. If only we knew what was ours to claim and enjoy.

FIRST-CLASS JOURNEY

In Czarist Russia, there was treachery and mass murder. The early twentieth century brought *Pogroms*, the systematic brutal destruction of entire villages. In the capital, there was an eleven-year-old boy named Alexander whose highly educated Jewish parents were members of the resistance. After his parents were executed, Alexander's grandmother smuggled him out of Russia and brought him north to Scandinavia to a port in Sweden. She used her life savings to buy Alexander a one-way, first-class ticket on a steam liner from Stockholm to New York Harbor. She wired ahead so relatives would be waiting for him in America. Before Alexander got on the massive ship that day, his grandmother hugged him and cried as if she would never see him again; indeed, she did not.

By the time he passed through the lines boarding the ship, he got shuffled in with many people. Before he knew it, he was placed in steerage for a two-and-a-half week journey. Steerage back in those days was not torture, but it wasn't very pleasant with its cramped quarters, whooping cough, poor ventilation, and bland food. After a few days, Alexander realized that nobody was looking for him, and nobody was looking after him, so he began to navigate his little body around the ship and take some short trips to the higher decks.

One day, Alexander secretly made his way to the end of the kitchen. Inquisitive, he stood on a crate to look through the round porthole of the swinging doors. He found himself peering into the first-class dining room. The sights and smells heightened his senses beyond what he thought possible. He stared. He salivated. He fantasized. He saw ice sculptures, mounds of bread, trays of fruit and cheeses, along with end-less platters of meat, fish, and fowl. He heard laughter and music. He watched the lovely, dressed-up women and hand-some gentlemen dancing.

Young Alexander was content to visit the kitchen and stand on the crate and crane his neck to vicariously experi-ence first-class dining every night for the rest of the voyage.

He continued to peer into that little round window to wish and imagine and hope.

When the ship docked in New York Harbor, there were a few distant relatives waiting for Alexander. They embraced him tightly and cried for the loss of his parents. As they began to ask him about his exciting voyage, it didn't take long for them to realize that something had gone very wrong. His descriptions of the conditions and the daily "trip" to the kitchen were not the stories they expected to hear from a boy whose grandmother had made such a sacrifice. "Alexander, show us the ticket! Where is your ticket?" He sheepishly dug deep into his pocket and produced the ticket. "Look, Alexander. This is a first-class ticket!"

Characteristic of an eleven-year-old boy, he shrugged his shoulders and shook his head. "I didn't know."

Aren't we a bit like Alexander? Through the ultimate sacrifice, Jesus provided us with a first-class ticket on this journey called life. Yet, we often get shuffled and disoriented and we settle for steerage. We settle for much less than He had planned for us. We crane our necks and look at other people's lives and we stare and make wishes and fantasize. *If only I could have that life, that talent, that house, that spouse, that job, that car, that family.* So many of us never come to fully enjoy the ride because we are so distracted by the scenery. God has provided safety and abundance. May we not come to the end of our journey feeling foolish about not enjoying what was generously given to us. I don't want to see God face to face only to apologetically offer an "I didn't know."

"Then you will know the truth, and the
truth will set you free."   (John 8:32)

LIVE YOUR BEST LIFE

Many people are in search of information. Oprah Winfrey has a virtual classroom of 22 million women, instructing them in how to "live your best life" through her impressive media empire. On the whole, our culture persuades us that our best life is only one infomercial away. Why are we tempted to believe we are always two "easy-pay" installments from looking younger and living better? No steps, secrets, or success program will ever give us our best life. In fact, there is not a more meaningful life than a God-driven life, and certainly no eternal life apart from Him. Living better is fine, but through His death and resurrection, Jesus made a way for us to live *forever*.

However, it's a leap of faith to believe all of this is true. It's considered by *some* to be narrow-minded, exclusionary, and illogical. And some have even labeled Christianity as patently offensive. For a Christian to say with a straight face, "Jesus is the only way," seems so extreme and unattractive in this "diverse, enlightened culture." That one would even have the audacity to suggest there is more to Christianity than living out a quiet, benign existence is often unsettling and threatening to those who are not in agreement. Sheila Walsh refers to Good Friday as "a scandalous, marvelous night." Two thousand years later, Jesus the Messiah is still causing quite a stir.

CHAPTER THREE

DESTINED FOR MORE

Y ou pray a long time for your husband to get closer to God, and then one day he becomes a fanatic. Frank came home from work soon after our second child was born and announced that in five years, we would go into full-time ministry.

"Honey, in a few years, we're going to sell everything and work full time for Jesus." What a noble thought.

I said, "Sure, that's great. That's nice. That's a good plan." What a special guy.

Well, he didn't seem too special when five years passed and he began to sell everything. The business, the small house we rented out, the lawnmower, the baby furniture. Reality had not yet set in when we put the house up for sale. Of course, Frank mentioned several times that our move would eventually happen, but I never thought it would *really* happen. After all, our content, blessed, fruitful life was in New York.

"Frank, Jesus needs missionaries right here in New York," I pleaded. "Surely, He can use us mightily right here in New

York, Frank. We don't need to move away. There are plenty of sinners in New York we could reach out to. Are you listening, Frank?"

My words fell on deaf (Spirit-directed) ears. After interviewing with some of the largest Christian ministries in the nation, Frank took a position with Charles Colson and Prison Fellowship Ministries near Washington, D.C. That was ten years ago.

When friends and church members heard we were leaving New York to enter full-time ministry in Virginia, they thought we were extraordinary and made many comments in that vein. They said things like, "Oh, isn't that wonderful that you will be reaching out to the least of these." I smiled at all the well-wishers and sheepishly received their praise.

I felt like the biggest con of all. In my heart, my thoughts were, "No, no, I'm not an exemplary Christian. I just live with Frank. *He* is the one who heard God." During the first three years of living in Virginia, I woke up each morning hoping I was back in New York. I miss Carvel. I miss provolone, copocola, mortadella, soppressata, and risotto. I miss Temptee cream cheese, and U-Bet chocolate syrup. I can't even get Drake's Cakes. I dream of Yodels and Devil Dogs. And last, but not at all least, I miss real pizza. I pine for pizza by the slice.

The day before we moved in1994, about 150 women and children from church stopped at our house for a "Bye-Bye" Bagel Brunch. I threw it for myself. It was the best way I could think of to see everyone I had come to love and appreciate through fifteen years of calling Smithtown Tabernacle our church home. It was a big tearjerker. I cried the most.

When I couldn't stand the compliments about my sacrifice and goodness any longer, I stood on the deck holding my smeared bagel and made my mammoth confession to my New York girlfriends: "Pray for me. I don't even care about prisoners. As a matter of fact, I think they should be in prison!" A hush fell over the yard, but thankfully they didn't take back the exquisitely designed, hand-etched vase they presented to me before we ate.

Where foot-in-mouth syndrome abounds, grace abounds all the more. Else Ebbestad sought me out and put her arms around me. She is an octogenarian from Norway who served on the mission field in Africa and Haiti for over forty years. It was a very special moment, considering she is one of my all-time heroes. Though Else is diminutive, I have looked up to her ever since Frank and I spent two weeks with her in Haiti twenty years ago. At the time of our move, Else had been visiting New York on sabbatical from Haiti, where she had lived among the poorest of the poor. And there I was, feeling sorry for myself and embarrassed all at once, knowing I was moving from one comfortable house in a New York City suburb to another comfortable house in a D.C. suburb. Else hugged me tight and assured me, "Home is wherever Jesus takes you."

The next few years were humbling and highly educational. I believe Bible teachers refer to it as "a season of pruning." I was pruned alright—down to my roots, which apparently were not as strong or as deep as I had presumed. Ouch, ouch, and ouch. The first humble pie I ate in its entirety was the one related to my attitude toward prisoners. Before we joined forces with the life-changing ministry of Prison Fellowship, I had not personally known a prisoner nor had I ever visited a prison. I had casually dismissed Christ's mandate to show concern for this portion of the population. After all, I was busy serving Jesus in *other* ways.

Enter the formidable Charles W. Colson. Although his involvement in the Watergate scandal placed him behind bars for seven months, Chuck asserts that God gave him a life sentence. For the past twenty-eight years, he has chosen to place himself inside prison walls around the globe. Since his incarceration, he has never spent a Resurrection Sunday outside of a prison. Chuck Colson is a true statesman, and I believe he will be regarded as one of the most influential Christian voices of the last quarter century. When Frank served as Vice President of the Prison Fellowship International Ministry, several of the Directors were former convicts. Please don't tell the relatives, but I would comfortably choose any of them as guardians for my children. They are husbands, fathers, and quite remarkable men of God. In fact, I have learned a lot about life from those who are familiar with prison cells.

I recently came across a letter that a woman had written from prison about how she felt her life was "about to begin." "When the kids are born ... ," she used to think, "That's when life will really begin." All too soon, however, it became, "When the kids grow up ... ." Then it was, "When we save enough money ... ." "When we pay off the house ... ." "When I finish my college degree."

She had come to a point of saying, "Here I am in prison.

And I really have to think about how I've wasted my life thinking some day it would begin for me when this or that happened." Her words are all too familiar to many of us. We fill in the blank with whatever makes us feel like someday we're going to be okay. Her prison exhortations are for all who have ears to hear.

Stop waiting until you ...
    finish school,
        go back to school,
            lose ten pounds,
                gain ten pounds,
                    have kids,
                        until the kids leave the house.
Stop looking for life to really begin when you ...
    start work,
        retire,
            get married,
                get divorced,
                  get a new home
                    or pay your home off.
Life is passing you by
    while you're patiently waiting
        for your song to come on
        or your ship to come in.

The fresh pursuit of who we really are in Christ—our destiny—begins today, not some far-off time in the future when we enter those pearly gates. Mother Teresa understood this well: "Yesterday is gone. Tomorrow has not yet come. We have only today. Let us begin." On the other hand, Janis Joplin, the controversial, highly celebrated rock icon of the sixties, offered her own version of this idea when she said, "Today is the first day of the rest of your life." Though she was not quoting Scripture, she was certainly quoting truth. Second Corinthians 5:17 tells us, "Therefore, if anyone is in Christ, he is a new creation; the old has gone, the new has come!" Sadly, Janis was unable to grasp this good news and lost her life to an addiction. If only she had known the deep joy and forgiveness of the One who desires to give us the life that overflows with intangible and priceless gifts. The rest of her life would have been vastly different.

Discovering our destiny in Christ is the difference between living the "good life" and experiencing the "real life" Jesus offers. We may think the good life begins the moment we finally receive what had seemed to be eluding us—getting the big promotion, becoming pregnant, paying off the house. In contrast, real life begins the moment we prioritize Jesus as our reason for living and passionately pursue His purposes. When we do this, we find that most of our earthly pursuits don't translate as "real living." Even at their best, these lesser things bring only temporary satisfaction to our souls.

Human beings have great instincts, and we've been endowed with incredible skills and gifts. Empires have been built, wars have been won, and millions have been made by people whose lives are devoid of devotion to God. There are many examples of people who do not profess faith and yet seem to be living out meaningful lives. They are in our offices, our neighborhoods, and our carpools. There are people all around us without faith in God who seem resilient and quite content. They somehow make it through difficulty and seem to be doing just fine. How can we justify that?

Jesus wasn't contradicting Himself when He explained that God "causes his sun to rise on the evil and the good, and sends rain on the righteous and the unrighteous" (Matt. 5:45). He was simply illustrating that God is a God of love who gives life to all human beings. Yet He gives *abundant* life to those who are willing to put their faith and trust in Him (John 10:10 NASB). Jesus was speaking of an abundance of the soul.

Those without a relationship to the Creator may be *living the good life* but still not be *fully alive*. Only God has promised us more. He takes human potential to the nth degree and puts us on the path to real living.

> Now you've got my feet on the life path,
> all radiant from the shining of your face.
> Ever since you took my hand,
> I'm on the right way.
> (Ps. 16:11 MSG)

ROAD MAP INCLUDED

There are some who say life is a gamble, a series of chances, a luck of the draw. I disagree. Although life is uncertain—God's faithfulness *is* certain. The believer in Christ can enjoy specific, reliable direction from a God who promises to give a lamp to our feet and a light to our path (Ps. 119:105). I like knowing that as I take His hand He leads me. When I was a seventh grader, I had a strong sense that I would someday be an English teacher. Miss Karla Kroll was my seventh grade English teacher. She was eloquent, witty, petite, animated, ebullient and very pretty. It didn't hurt that she had short, thick, curly hair, just like mine. I later realized that God had planted that seed in my heart and watered it faithfully in the ten years that followed.

In 1975, His still small voice pointed me toward Boston College. I pursued my teaching degree with great fervor and I continued to make my relationship with Jesus a priority. I involved myself in several facets of campus ministry. I was trained to be a Eucharistic Minister and sang songs and played guitar every Saturday night for midnight mass held in the dorms. Every Sunday morning, I hopped the trolley to head downtown to Ruggles Street Church where I first entered into regular, systematic study of the Word. Although I had a healthy social life, I once again sensed God's clear direction for my future. This time, it was concerning a mate. I dated a few guys, but it seemed to me that Prince Charming was not on my campus. It was a helpful realization which spared me heartache (and money on Valentine's Day!).

Though I received numerous job offers near Boston, I chose to return to New York after graduation to teach at William Floyd High School. A wonderful man named Frank Lofaro was waiting there for me on Long Island. I could have happily, comfortably taken a teaching position up in Boston, but I didn't. Isn't that amazing how life's twists and turns can change our course in such powerful and eternal ways?

After we married, I "knew" we would have children. Our three children are named Paris (for the City of Light), Jordan (for the River of Life), and Capri (for the Isle of Love).

As the role of wife and mother unfolded, which is a high calling in and of itself, I sensed God saying to me, "I want to make you a better communicator, one who will challenge and encourage others in their faith." And God has been faithful to bring opportunities my way, including the most unexpected and delightful surprises, in order to fulfill what He called me to do.

Destiny is about doing and being all God wants you to do and be. Living your best life is not Oprah Winfrey's idea. It was God's! "I came so they can have real and eternal life, more and better life than they ever dreamed of" (John 10:10 MSG). Seeing yourself as a winner is not Tony Robbins' idea. It was God's! "In all these things we are more than conquerors through him who loved us" (Rom. 8:37). Enjoying financial freedom, believe it or not, is not original to Suze Orman. It was God's idea! "Bring your full tithe ... so there will be ample provisions in my Temple. Test me in this and see if I don't open up heaven itself to you and pour out blessings beyond your wildest dreams" (Mal. 3:10 MSG). God's blessings, God's riches, God's provisions—both seen and unseen—are ours.

"I can do everything through him who gives me strength" (Phil. 4:13). Do we really comprehend the promise that nothing is impossible with God? God raised Jesus from the dead! All things are now possible. The leap of faith is to believe that being a Christian is way beyond "just getting in."

We are ordinary people, but we have an extraordinary God, and He does amazing things. *All* the time.

THE REST IS DETAILS

I appreciate when major companies or small businesses place their mission statement over the door, in the lobby, and on the phone recording when they place you on hold. Have you called GE lately? The prerecorded message is almost as moving as a Hallmark commercial. I was on hold with Southwest Airlines recently and the message said, "You're not on hold. Rather, think of yourself as being held." *Being held?* I was choked up by all the love. Going to a tire store these days can be quite an uplifting experience. While I waited to have a flat fixed, I noticed the strategically placed signs emoting: "Let us serve you." "We want to care for you." "You are important to us." I was overwhelmed by all the profuse honesty, kindness, and integrity. A lot of these mission statements seem very spiritual, and you feel like there must surely be a Christian in the back somewhere. But that's not necessarily the case.

My personal mission statement is very brief, because twenty-two years of marriage to a concise, precise man has helped me understand that longwinded people aren't invited back. So here it is: "To know Him and to make Him known." That's it. Frank arranges quarterly meetings (the children are forced to attend) and everyone is asked the same question: "How are you doing on the Lofaro family mission statement?" We have told the kids their main goal and reason for living is to know Jesus and to make Him known. The rest is details.

"You could be a movie star; you could be a street cleaner," we tell our kids. "You could work with the poor; you could work on Wall Street. You could join the Army; you could join the Salvation Army. You could live at the beach; you could live at The White House." Whatever you do to earn a living is a detail that will never match the importance of the One you serve. In the words of Bob Dylan, "It may be the devil, or it may be the Lord—but ya gotta serve somebody."

What is *your* mission statement? What are *you* here for? If we don't know what we're here for, there are a lot of good reasons to go to happy hour. If we don't know what we're here for, there are a lot of good reasons to worry about what is and isn't in the bank. If we don't know what we're here for, there are a lot of good reasons to fear the newscasts, El Niño, mad cows, mad terrorists, and mad relatives. If I didn't know that God is watching over me, I would be a nervous wreck. If I didn't believe in eternal life, I would probably live this life differently. The hedonist philosophy of "He who dies with the most toys wins" might make some sense if dirt was my final frontier.

God sent His only Son to change all that. Jesus is the Prince of Peace. He is the source of true and lasting joy. His death and resurrection are the bridge to eternal life. His promise to us is our reason for living.

THE PROMISE REVEALS HIS PURPOSE

God reveals His promises so that we understand the difference between merely existing and living for a purpose. Between surviving and thriving.

His promise captures all you are meant to be. I love what Max Lucado says in his book, *Just Like Jesus.* [5] "God loves you just the way you are, but too much to leave you that way." The Bible teaches that we are "fearfully and wonderfully made," and that the work of His hands is decidedly "wonderful" (Ps. 139:14). Yet God's wildest dream for us is that one day we will be just like His Son, Jesus.

His promise captures all you are meant to do. God's promises come with instructions. He has a plan for our lives that He wants us to follow. The Bible tells us Jesus prays for us the way we pray for our own loved ones. "Therefore he is able to save completely those who come to God through him, because he always lives to intercede for them" (Heb. 7:25). And in the same way that we can't control other people's choices, He loves us enough to allow us free will. Will it break my heart if our kids choose poorly in life? Yes, but will I forgive them? A healthy parent will. Will it break God's heart if we divert from His plan? Yes, but God is the perfect parent who willingly forgives and restores us. His plan is to take paupers like us and lavish His promises upon us. To make us princes and princesses. He wants to bless us. Why? Just because He loves and adores us. That's it. Blessing us gives Him joy.

THE PROMISE REVEALS HIS CHARACTER

There are people in our homes, at work, behind the pulpit, on the air, and over the internet who have made some impressive promises. Some of them are telling us the truth, and some of them are not. We often decide what we are willing to believe based on the character of those making the promises. Are they credible? Are they trustworthy? Have they let us down before?

If a promise gains its value from the one making the promise, then God's promises are priceless. In fact, the reason why He makes and keeps a promise is in order to reveal His character. He promises us good things to teach us that He is good. He promises us unconditional love to show us that He is love. However, our human experience may have discolored our perception of God. As a result, our understanding of His promises may be warped as well. When you think of God's promises to you, what comes to mind? It's not always easy to answer that question. Do you feel that God has promised you health, wealth, and happiness? How about an attractive spouse? A white picket fence? Weight loss?

A. W. Tozer, the author of the classic book *Pursuit of God* once said, "What comes into your mind when you think about God is the most important thing about you." Is God a bellhop? A heavenly sadist? A cosmic killjoy with a slingshot waiting to pick you off? Is He waiting for your number to come up, so you can get cancer? Is He an accountant keeping tabs on what you did when you were seventeen? A geriatric God who's sitting on a rocker, dozing off from time to time? An angry God? An uninvolved God? Or … is He a saving God? A loyal friend? A passionate, giving, kind God who is *for* you, not against you?

Many people who wouldn't set foot inside a church go to sleep at night wishing someone would care for them, deeply and unconditionally. They want someone to look out for them and take an interest in their lives. They may not be ready to call God by name, but something inside is starting to tell them that the God they're looking for may be closer than they ever imagined possible. Meditate on God's promises here below as a fresh reminder or a new revelation of the kind of God you always dreamed you'd find. (Italics added.)

> Know therefore that the LORD your God is God; he is the *faithful* God, keeping his covenant of love to a thousand generations of those who love him and keep his commands.
> —Deuteronomy 7:9

> For the word of the LORD is right and true; he is *faithful* in all he does.
> —Psalm 33:4

> The Maker of heaven and earth, the sea, and everything in them— the LORD, who remains *faithful* forever.
> —Psalm 146:6

> Great is your *faithfulness*.
> —Lamentations 3:23

> The one who calls you is *faithful* and he will do it.
> —1 Thessalonians 5:24

If we confess our sins, he is *faithful* and just
and will forgive us our sins and purify us from
all unrighteousness.

—1 John 1:9

THE PROMISE REVEALS HIS PROVISION

God's promise also tells us what and how He has provided for us. According to Psalm 50:10, our heavenly Father owns the "cattle on a thousand hills." Therefore, certain privileges are just a given. We don't have to beg for our needs to be met. We are His concern, and taking care of us is His responsibility and pleasure. If my children were to slither to the breakfast table in the morning with their heads down and groveling, "Oh, Mother, dear Mother, if we couldst have Frosted Flakes, though we do not deserveth them, how lovely that would be. If thou hast a moment to give us a mere Pop-Tart crumb, we wouldst be forever in your debt."

Do you know what I would say? "Get up, you silly kids! Get off that floor! What are you doing? Sit down at the table. It's there for the taking." How God must look at us with the same puzzled expression as we cower before Him, asking for a moment of His time to whisper our requests. God is not impressed with our lowliness. I think He must be sad when we beg for that which He longs to give. Surely He doesn't wish for us to approach Him like a distant taskmaster. We are not paupers or homeless orphans; we are children of the King. "How great is the love the Father has lavished on us, that we should be called children of God! And that is what we are!" (1 John 3:1). God says to us, "You're my child. Everything I have is yours. Come to the table and partake."

Contemporary Christian musician Steven Curtis Chapman and his wonderful wife, Mary Beth, adopted an orphaned baby girl from China. Steven is a highly talented and deeply principled man of God. His gifts and talents have brought many seen and unseen rewards; he is considered a major success in the Christian music industry. By the world's standards, the Chapmans are well off. When they arrived in China to meet little Shaohannah Hope and sign the adoption papers, two very important things happened simultaneously. Shaoey became a Chapman and she also became entitled to all Steven and Mary Beth's worldly possessions. What did she do to earn it? What did she do to deserve it? What would she have to do to hold onto it? The answer to each of these questions is: "Not a thing." When Shaoey received a new name, she also received a new inheritance. Their dramatically, life-changing adoption experience was so wonderful that they welcomed a second Chinese baby girl into their home. The arrival of Stevey Joy makes them a very complete family of seven. Along with two precious babies, God has sent the Chapman family unspeakable "hope" and "joy."

I'm not in the habit of feeding the neighbors' children each night at dinnertime. I'm not sending any of them to college. And I do not buy them new school clothes. However, I'm taking very good care of the three who bear the Lofaro name. God sees you as His adopted child—grafted into His family tree. Everything He has is yours. Romans chapter four assures us that God's promises are not lost in Old Testament lore. In fact, the Bible says His promises are "guaranteed to all Abraham's offspring ... he is the father of us all" (Rom. 4:16). And it gets better. "You are all sons of God through faith in Christ Jesus, for all of you who were baptized into Christ have clothed yourselves with Christ ... If you belong to Christ, then you are Abraham's seed, and heirs according to the promise" (Gal. 3:26–27, 29). "So those who have faith are blessed along with Abraham, the man of faith" (Gal. 3:9).

I enjoyed the rich opportunity of being raised in a predominantly Jewish neighborhood on Long Island. I didn't quite understand anti-Semitism. If anything, I had Jewish-envy. On Long Island, all my Jewish friends had such incredible family ties. Success was valued in Jewish homes in a way I didn't see in *goyim* homes. I used to yearn for the cohesiveness I saw and for the sense of "favor" I saw on their lives. Isn't this what we all want? A sense that we belong to something and someone? For blessing and favor to fall upon our shoulders wherever we go? This is the sense of adoption we feel when we realize our position in God's family. We're not outsiders enviously looking in on all that God has for other people. In fact, the Bible says, "Consequently, you are no longer foreigners and aliens, but fellow citizens with God's people and members of God's household" (Eph. 2:19). Do you know God's promises for you? Are you aware of all you have in Christ? Don't be a stranger to God's promises; it's time you started enjoying them. Let's begin by looking at the four promises He gave to Abraham.

PART
TWO

CHAPTER FOUR

GOD'S PROMISES

The LORD had said to Abram, "Leave your country,
your people and your father's household and go to the
land I will show you. I will make you into a great nation
and I will bless you; I will make your name great, and
you will be a blessing. I will bless those who bless you, and
whoever curses you I will curse; and all peoples on earth
will be blessed through you."

(Gen. 12:1–3)

Imagine Abram receiving this incredible message from God out of the blue one day. Now imagine Abram announcing this news to his wife later on that same day as she's fixing dinner.

"That's nice, honey. Which god? And what did he have to say?"

"It was *the* God and He said He's going to give us property, prosperity, and make us a people" (spoken with growing excitement). "He's going to do great things for us and through us."

(Sarai has yet to look up from the stove.)

"One more thing, hon. He said we have to leave all this behind and that He has new property for us."

"Oh, that's terrific. Where is it?"

There's the rub. Abram doesn't know where. God left out that part. Abram and Sarai have a good life living near Abram's family. It's comfortable and his father, Terah, has real estate. Abe's got history, hierarchy, and heritage. His roots are there. But God steps onto the scene with a sweeping promise to give Abram more than he ever imagined if he is willing to follow.

Realizing that "going without knowing" is hard for us humans to handle, God gave him some more encouragement. "After this the word of the Lord came to Abram in a vision, saying, 'Do not be afraid, Abram. I am your shield, your very great reward'" (Gen. 15:1).

Even amid the uncertainty, there was joy in Abram's household that day. God had promised him incredible things. He would be great. He would have a future. He would be the father of a nation of people who would grow to love and serve God. God gave Abram a new start in life and gave him a new name.

> "No longer will you be called Abram; your name will be Abraham, for I have made you a father of many nations. I will make you very fruitful; I will make nations of you, and kings will come from you. I will establish my covenant as an everlasting covenant between me and you and your descendants after you for the generations to come, to be your God and the God of your descendants after you. The

whole land of Canaan, where you are now an alien, I will give as an everlasting possession to you and your descendants after you; and I will be their God." (Gen. 17:5–8)

God's promises inspired Abraham to trust Him and move forward into all that God had in mind for him. Not satisfied to merely accept all that was, Abraham was ready for a leap of faith, pushing himself toward all that was to come.

PROPERTY

"I will give you this land ... " Let's put our ear to the tent again and pick up that conversation going on between Abraham and his wife.

"Where are we going, Abe?"

"Oh, I didn't ask where. God just said we were going somewhere good."

"But we just settled down here. I just got into a new car pool. We're close to a good school. We can't just pick up and go—we haven't even seen this new place."

And yet Abraham hears God speaking his new name. "Abraham, I have property you have yet to see."

Has God been telling you He wants to give you some new land? Of course, it may not be a physical place, but maybe it's a territory concerning your future dreams and aspirations. Is He prodding you to reach for a place you have yet to see in your spiritual life? God wants to bring us to that place, even if we can't even see what it looks like yet.

Frank and I attended an anniversary celebration for our former home church in Long Island. Sitting there in the beautiful 2000-seat sanctuary and watching a slide show of Norwegians digging with shovels in 1948 made me stop and reflect. A group of young Norwegian missionaries left the comforts of home and went to New York to minister to Norwegian sailors on the docks of Brooklyn. They built Salem Tabernacle and then some of them believed God for property on Long Island in 1948. They met at a VFW hall and eventually bought a small plot of land where they started digging a hole in the ground.

Is God still offering us property today? I believe God wants to stake all kinds of property for His name's sake in and around my present "hometown" of Reston, Virginia, as well as in yours. What lands do you wish to discover and "conquer" with His help? He wants to cross over into every land and claim it for our use and His glory. Rehab centers, halfway houses, crisis pregnancy centers, homeless shelters, senior centers, churches—all of these bring the land to life. For example, there's something uniquely appealing about a well-maintained, after-school ministry or youth center in the middle of a rundown neighborhood. In the midst of a concrete jungle, it's invigorating to see a flowerbed and fresh paint. When land becomes attractive and beautiful, it offers something to everyone who passes by. There is color. Laughter. Life eminates in every direction.

God told Abraham, "Lift up your eyes from where you are and look north and south and east and west. All the land that you see I will give to you and your offspring forever" (Gen. 13:14–15). In our modern American culture, most of us live in the sprawling urban centers and suburbs. We've lost much of the beauty, both profound and simple, of the agricultural lifestyle. Too often, we don't fully appreciate the analogy and imagery of land, seeds, fields, and harvest. The Bible often refers to the planting, sowing, and reaping process and portrays blessing by describing a full crop and ripe fields. Our responsibility is to tend the fields and care for the land He has given to us.

And yet property can also be abused. There is nothing more disconcerting than an abandoned, run-down building or a neglected piece of property that has been turned into a dumping ground. During one of our many visits back to New York, Frank and I decided to visit the place where we held our wedding reception twenty years earlier. The kids were with us, so we were excited to reminisce and show the place off.

When we wed, Frank and I attempted to celebrate our union in a unique way. Rather than using a typical catering hall, we celebrated at the Wellwyn Estate—a grand mansion of postcard perfection, situated on a north shore bluff, facing Long Island Sound. Imagine our shock and disappointment years later when we drove up the circular drive to find a dilapidated house, a dead garden, overgrown brush, and piles of debris—which included stained carpeting, broken furniture, and stacks of splintered trellis. Our picture perfect wedding mansion looked like a haunted house! Our "witty" children made some wisecracks and Frank and I smiled and laughed along, trying to be good sports. In all honesty, it hurt a little to see it in such poor condition. We were disappointed that the once gracious property was in such disrepair, and I for one wished we had not seen the unfortunate results. Frank and I talked more about our disappointing detour later that night and we thanked the Lord that, unlike the neglected property, our marriage had strengthened and grown more lovely over the years.

The idea of tending the land also refers to our responsibility to care for the "land" within ourselves, the holy ground the Spirit within us calls home. "Do you not know that your body is a temple of the Holy Spirit, who is in you, whom you have received from God?" (1 Cor. 6:19). Some of us are well-groomed on the outside but we have neglected the inside of our "temple." We have maintained the physical landscape and we look good on the outside, but in a spiritual sense we have "let ourselves go." How can we tend to the world when we haven't tended to ourselves? There may have been a time in our spiritual history when vitality and passion filled our lives, but today observers would find that hard to imagine. When our devotion becomes dilapidated, there is little about us to attract others to our faith.

Our children, our friends, and our family are also forms of "land" (relational geography, if you will). God gives us these relationships with the expectation that we will tend to them like a dedicated farmer tends a crop, hoping to reap a harvest from his hard work. Jesus used this imagery when He talked about seizing opportunities to share our faith with others. "Do you not say, 'Four months more and then the harvest'? I tell you, open your eyes and look at the fields! They are ripe for harvest" (John 4:35). Survey the land around you and open your eyes to the potential for harvest in your relationships at home, at the office, and in your neighborhood and community.

PROMINENCE

"I will make your name great ... " I have the privilege of sharing friendship and church membership with the former Washington Redskin Darrell Green and his wife, Jewell. Our teenage daughters are close friends. When Frank and I received an invitation to Darrell's surprise fortieth birthday party, I knew it would be a very special event. It was a black tie gala held at a beautiful hotel. It was obvious that Jewell, who also happens to be an interior designer, had gone all out. The fabulous décor, the very cool ensemble, the sumptuous food, the pre-dining movie theatre experience (complete with huge posters, popcorn carts, great candy, and special footage starring The Man), were every bit as impressive as the NFL and media guest list. Yet what I'll remember much more than *any* of those wonderful things were the words Darrell shared at the end of the evening. He delivered the Gospel unapologetically, purely, and straightforwardly. And what objections came from the non-Christians and the self-reliant millionaires in that ballroom? There were *none*. Why? Because Darrell Green had done his job well for twenty years. He had earned the right to speak as he wished.

Many celebrities use their platforms to advance personal profit as well as noble causes. To me, Darrell was so much more than a talented, well-loved, forty-year-old NFL star that night. He took time during an exquisite party to advance the kingdom. He deflected the praise and pointed every person to the King. Now, that's a true prince.

Those who are "great" in the fields of sports, entertainment, and business are highly esteemed and handsomely rewarded. We know many of their names by heart—Jordan, Cruise, and Gates. But that's where human greatness and kingdom greatness differ. When committed believers excel at whatever it is they do, the praise ultimately goes to only one name—Jesus. He receives the praise, honor, and glory that He is fully worthy to receive. This is the way we begin to truly impact a world in need of a sovereign Savior.

The carefully constructed Tower of Babel in Genesis 11 was intended to herald human achievement. "Then [the people] said, 'Come, let us build ourselves a city, with a tower that reaches to the heavens, so that we may make a name for ourselves'" (Gen. 11:4). However, God made sure that self-aggrandizing building project soon came to a halt. We don't become great in order to make a name for ourselves. God makes people great in order to magnify *His* name. God told Abraham He would make his name great for His sake. In essence, God said to Abraham, "I will make your name great because you believe in me." It was God's pleasure to honor the one who honored Him.

I believe this message of greatness is something Christians need to hear. It reminds me of the commercial for an investment firm with sepia-toned headshots of little kids talking about what they want to do when they grow up. "I want to be overworked and underpaid," one boy says with a serious face. Another girl announces, "I want to be devalued. I want to be treated poorly because I'm a woman." Another states, "I want to be excessed at an early age." What irony! None of us start out in life saying things like that. In fact, we have a culture that applauds and rewards greatness. Yet, somewhere along the way, we begin to believe greatness is for someone else. So we settle for less than what we were created to be.

Are you involved with Creative Memories? Be great at it. You're an accountant? Be great. You're a mother wiping little behinds all day? Do it well. Whatever it is you're doing in life, be great. I'm not very domestically gifted. When I scream, "DINNER!!!" my children run to the car. But what I do well, I want to do *very* well. I don't want to be a mediocre communicator; I want to be great. For my glory? No, for God's. He's watching, and I want to make Him proud.

When others mention our name or our family's name they should be able to say with admiration, "That's a great family. That's a fine mother. What a good father he is to the kids." Be great in art, be great in cooking, be great in computers, be great in business, be a great teacher, a great nurse, a great neighbor, a great daughter-in-law, a great brother. Be great, and do not settle for less, because God deserves the very best we have to offer Him.

In the Age of Enlightenment, people began to think of themselves more highly than they ought. We still do that as a result of our self-absorption and humanistic ideology which promotes humans to deity status. In the Christian mindset, the pendulum has swung too far the other way at times, and we are uncomfortable with so much as a compliment. Have you been at a church service to honor someone and every other sentence is a disclaimer about not glorifying any person? Some seem to think that we must deflect every sincere compliment issued in our favor.

Yet God clearly exalts people and lifts them up. He gives

us reputations in order to be godly, wise, great, and have an impact on others. Sometimes I catch myself deflecting praise after a weekend retreat or daylong conference. When women hug me and tell me how I touched their lives, I generally have an automatic holy response. "Oh no, sister, God did it all. I'm just a vessel." Nothing like making someone feel foolish. Of *course* I'm the vessel. I don't even *look* like God. I am trying to be better about saying, "Thank you—I thank the Lord with you."

"Greatness" describes many of our very human Old and New Testament heroes. It's okay to speak highly and fondly about biblical *and* modern Christian heroes. We have many wonderful role models in the Scriptures, but rest assured that God did not stop producing them after John penned Revelation. We should look to the saints, both in heaven and on earth, and emulate those who have provided us with their powerful testimony. However, many don't see how "that kind of holy" fits into a twenty-first-century lifestyle. We've made them more like icons than real-life examples. "Mother Teresa was holy, but I'm not going to look good with that white thing around my head. So forget it!" we may say to ourselves. So we tend to lower the bar and settle for less than holy role models.

Too many believers (yes, especially women) seem to have come to the conclusion that they are as important as worms. Remember the scene of my children crawling to the table to beg for scraps? "Oh, Lord, I really hate to bother you, but if you have any time today, I just heard that I have breast cancer, and I was wondering if I could have a minute. I know you're busy in the Middle East, but could you please maybe possibly let me know when you can fit me in?" Or maybe your plea is, "My spouse is leaving me, so when you have some time ..." Or, "My kids are screaming, and I'm screaming, and, God, if maybe, just maybe, you could take some time to help ... ?"

He loves us so uniquely and has designed a destiny for us with bountiful blessings. And yet we often think God's time and His promises are for someone else. Someone who doesn't have the history we do. Someone who has it more together. Someone. Anyone. Just not us. Some of us can't imagine that God could ever use us for His eternal purposes. The enemy will tell you that you'll never measure up, never make a difference, and never get to heaven. If you've ever felt that way, I have great news for you. God called upon many individuals who had lots of "issues." So, why would He ever call on you? You're in good company!

Moses stuttered. David's armor didn't fit. John Mark was rejected by Paul. Timothy had ulcers. Hosea's wife was a prostitute. Amos's only training was in the school of fig-tree pruning. Jacob was a liar. David had an affair. Solomon was too rich. Jesus was too poor. Abraham was too old. David was too young. Peter was afraid of death. Lazarus *was* dead! John was self-righteous. Naomi was a widow. Paul was a murderer; Moses was, too. Jonah ran from God. Miriam was a gossip. Gideon doubted. Jeremiah was a bullfrog. *Just seeing if you were paying attention.* But he *was* depressed and suicidal. Elijah was burned out. John the Baptist was a loudmouth. Martha was a worrywart. Mary was lazy. Samson had long hair. Noah got drunk.

So, *why* would God call you? Because He desires to bless you abundantly despite the reasons you are so sure He can't use you.

PROSPERITY

"I will bless you ... and you will be a blessing ..." God instructed Abraham that he would not only have enough for himself and his family; he would also bless his community and even an entire nation. From the story of Joseph and the famine through the New Testament account of the loaves and fishes, God fulfilled His promise that His people would prosper and enjoy His abundant blessings.

Unfortunately, the concept of prosperity can be misunderstood. I'm not suggesting that God wants you to own a Mercedes-Benz. When I visited Haiti (the poorest country in the western hemisphere) to help build a church and school, I noticed the Haitian Christians were "prospering" in the midst of extreme poverty. Let me explain. They were well-groomed, nicely dressed, full of joy, and displayed greater dignity and a more peaceful demeanor than the locals who chose to maintain their voodoo practices. What made the difference? Certainly not the quality of rice and produce available. Both groups were living in the same conditions and experiencing the same economy. What caused the difference? Being part of the body of Christ changes things. Church life changes things. Sharing and caring changes things. I was in a poverty-stricken place, but I witnessed the proof, power, and promise of genuine and pure prosperity.

In God's economy, prosperity is not as much about dollars and cents as it is spiritual richness. The Bible contrasts the world's idea of wealth saying, "But godliness with contentment is great gain. For we brought nothing into the world, and we can take nothing out of it. But if we have food and clothing, we will be content with that" (1 Tim. 6:6–8). Contentment, peace, gratitude—all of these comprise spiritual richness. A prosperous heart is a grateful one and doesn't pine for what it doesn't have. I can't obtain all of my "wants." God lovingly withholds some of them from me so He can meet my greater "needs" instead. Gaining this kind of perspective and wisdom is *indeed* essential to prospering.

Want to discover just how wealthy you are? Take inventory of all you have, and begin developing a thankful heart. Colossians 2:6–7 tells us to have a heart overflowing with thanks. Even in the midst of heartache, there is much in this life for which we need to be thankful. Jesus left the wealth of heaven in order to don a robe and some sandals, but He continued to give thanks at all times. He publicly thanked the Father in advance for what He would accomplish through the many miracles. He thanked God for the privilege of hearing His prayer before He called Lazarus from the grave. At the Last Supper with His disciples, He gave thanks for the simple meal of bread and drink.

In contrast to Jesus' wealth of gratitude—despite all the heavenly riches He had forsaken by coming to earth—we often have poor attitudes. We want to see what we get first, and then we'll decide if we need to be thankful. Philippians 4:6 reminds us to present our requests to God "with thanksgiving." The

Bible teaches us to thank God *in advance* for what He is going to do. In this way, thankfulness is an exercise of faith—believing what we don't yet see.

No wonder thankfulness is one of the most difficult character traits to develop. William Bennett, author of *The Book of Virtues*, describes a thankful heart and the difficulty we have in teaching our children what it means to be grateful. We will constantly meet with disappointment if we think we have something more coming to us. Maybe you've seen this in children when they go on vacation. *"This* is the hotel we're staying in?" Or after the euphoria of unwrapping gifts has all-too-soon faded, "Is *this* all I'm getting for Christmas?" If we don't develop gratitude early on, a keen sense of disappointment carries throughout our lives as we move further and further away from what it really means to be prosperous. "Oh, *this* is where you want me to work? ... Oh, *this* is the spouse you have picked out for me? Oh ... (*fill in your own favorite complaint*)." We have become an "I deserve" generation instead of being a grateful one for all the riches—seen and unseen—that God has given to us.

PEOPLE

"I will make you into a great nation ... " When Frank and I left the beautiful new sanctuary on Long Island after the anniversary celebration, we realized it wasn't just property the church founders trusted God for—it was also people. People to fill the property. That church was our home for fifteen years, and it has touched hundreds of thousands of lives

with the Gospel. God told Abraham, "I'm going to give you people. You're going to have children. So many, they're innumerable. Try counting the stars, and if that doesn't paint a clear word picture, head to the seashore and start counting the grains of sand. You're going to have many descendants."

Today more people, especially women, have graduate degrees than at any other time in our nation's history. People have talents; they have positions. They have faux painting in the right places in their homes. But somewhere along the path to success, they decided that God is not a priority. Spirituality is chic, but many are "done" with God and religion. After confirmation, after the wedding, at the cemetery, in divorce court, in the hospital … somewhere … sometime … they became angry, busy, or disillusioned and decided God didn't matter anymore.

Yet everybody wants "spirituality," and to be sure, there are plenty of "spirits" pervading the culture. However, people need to experience the Holy Spirit of God. They need Jesus. His job is to cultivate our character so we can influence other people with the good news of the Gospel. The Bible describes it as developing the fruit of the Spirit (Gal. 5:22–26). It is so exciting to have the privilege to present the good news of God's promise to others. God has promised you people—are you taking Him up on the promise?

CHAPTER FIVE

FROM FEAR TO FAITH

It was a chilly Friday night at the Star Lake Salvation Army Conference Center in north Jersey. November 1, 2002, to be exact. I had concluded teaching the first of four sessions for a women's retreat. It was great to be back north where the majority of the "sistas" had my dark hair color and my accent. The retreat committee arranged for a lovely dessert social in the dining hall and after I filled my plate, I meandered through the large room and spotted a table of blondes. (Since writing my second book, *Bonding with the Blonde Women*, I am fully healed and am now actually *drawn* to blonde women.) I asked if I could occupy the empty chair. It didn't take more than a minute for me to look at all six faces and realize they were related. They had that "family face." They already knew who *I* was so I took on my talk show host persona and asked a few dozen questions. Name. Age. Career. Marital status. Reason for coming on the weekend. Whether or not anyone was coerced. Why they smile so much. Where they live. (No, I never asked anyone's weight. Characteristic of most blonde women, they were all thinner than me, so I didn't go there.)

In just thirty minutes, I learned that the four natural blondes were the Donohue sisters and the two bottle blondes were the girls' mother and aunt, Pat Donohue and Pat's sister, Sharon Flynn. They all originally hail from a suburb of Boston and are now spread across the country. Kara, Annie, Kelly, and Erin live in four different states. Kara Donohue Nadeau, the oldest at thirty-four, was a former financial industry wiz, a wife, and a mother. It was Kara's church that sponsored the retreat. The four sisters beamed somewhat proudly as each one spoke. They laughed easily and gazed upon one another with loving admiration and a closeness that is rare. This was clearly a special family and when I asked Pat what she did "right" to raise such fine women, she chuckled and blushed and shrugged and seemed to deflect any glory. The out-of-towners informed me that they decided to come to the retreat to all be together and to spend some quality time with Kara's sons, David and Teddy, whom they miss and adore. Our table talk was delightful and I thanked them for allowing me to feel so welcome.

At the top of the stairs, the committee chairwoman stopped me before I entered my room. "Ellie, what prompted you to sit at *that* table?" I knew she was familiar with the title of my last book. "Oh, Peggy, I don't know. I'm just trying to reach out more to blonde women." We giggled, more from exhaustion than anything else. I regained some composure. "Actually, it was the Lord. I was so touched by their kindness and tender love toward one another. Where can I sign up for my kids to turn out like that?"

Peggy's face grew a bit pained. "Ellie, did you meet Kara?"

"Yes, as a matter of fact I did. I think she was the ringleader. Isn't she the one who attends Hawthorne Gospel?"

Peggy grimaced. "Kara had breast cancer two years ago and it has now spread throughout her body. She was given six months at most to live. Kara wanted her family to experience a Christian retreat with her. They're here to honor her and grant one of her last wishes."

My heart sank. I hugged Peggy goodnight, entered my room, and put on my pajamas. I went over my notes for the morning and prayed and laid there for an hour. My spirit was heavy and my thoughts were racing. *Terminal cancer? Six months to live? Only thirty-four? A two and four year old? She seemed so peaceful. She doesn't even look sick. She actually has a glow. Will she die, Lord?*

I could not turn my brain off, so being the shy, passive New Yorker I am, I went down the hall in my Lucille Ball style flannels and started knocking on doors in search of Kara. I was determined to find her. I needed to talk. After a few wrong doors, I finally found the right room. I knocked and Kara's sister Annie answered by cracking the door open a few inches. She looked at me with utter surprise (or was it some *other* emotion?) and swiftly closed the door. I heard the crumbling of snack bags and remembered the announcement banning food in the rooms. Annie sounded muffled: "It's the speaker!"

Kara's voice retorted, "Well, hide those chips and let her in!"

I pressed my lips up against the doorframe, "Yeah, I'm hungry—let me in!" Annie acquiesced and I was soon sitting

Indian style at the end of Kara's single bed. Kara sat up, leaning back against the headboard and Annie sat five feet away in the middle of her own single bed. They raised their eyebrows and grinned widely, waiting for *me* to say something. After all, it's not every day some middle-aged woman wearing pajamas pops in after midnight to strike up conversation with near strangers.

I told them what I had heard from Peggy and I told them about my restlessness and my pained heart. I then asked Kara to tell *me* some things. Like how it all works. What it feels like. Whom she talks to. Where she goes to cry. What she had done to be healed. Whether she gets mad at God. She was gracious, radiant, magnetic, and loving. Kara spoke openly and honestly and with a supernatural peace. She spoke of the grueling treatments and explained how it was decided that she would stop receiving them. She spoke of how she is preparing the boys—how she is handling mortality—and how it had affected her faith, her marriage, and her view of heaven. She even told me what plans she had made for her own funeral. She sat up a bit taller and gleefully shared that her cancer had brought Annie into a relationship with God. Annie nodded in agreement and explained that witnessing Kara's joy and peace in the midst of pain and suffering made her come to the conclusion that Kara's God *had* to be real. Kara made calls and located a vibrant church and a Bible study near Annie's home.

Kara heaved a deep sigh and uttered words that seemed nonsensical. "I can honestly say that I thank God for the cancer. It has brought me closer to the Lord. I have a deeper understanding of His faithfulness. It has opened many doors for me to share my faith. Annie is a now a believer and I am trusting that my entire family will be together for all eternity. David and the boys are going to be all right. God loves them and will meet all their needs. I wouldn't have chosen this path, but I do choose to trust God completely."

By now, my eyes were filled past the brims and the tears began to trickle. Like Annie, I knew that I, too, had witnessed a remarkable peace and that I would never quite be the same. I hugged my two hostesses goodnight, tucked each of them in, turned off the lamp, and bent over to kiss Kara's forehead. When I opened the door to leave, I turned for a moment and looked back into the small, darkened room. "Kara, I speak to so many women who fear death and dying. What's the *one thing* I should tell them? What's the *one thing* you have learned through all the suffering?"

Kara's answer returned swiftly and purposefully from out of the dark. She had obviously thought of it long before that night. "Tell them, 'You can't pin your hopes on living.'"

I wanted to make sure I had heard her correctly. *"You can't pin your hopes on living?"*

"Yep. You can't pin your hopes on living. Not in *this* world."

I whispered back toward the dark, "G'night." and returned to my room.

Where are you pinning *your* hopes? A paid-off mortgage? A healthy diet? An impressive financial portfolio? A highly rated hospital? We white-knuckle our way through this life because this life is all we know. Through His Son, Jesus, God provided a life that will *never* end. I am quite sure *that's* the life where we are to pin all our hopes. Jesus said He has gone to prepare a place for us. He said we'll receive our reward there and that we should lay up for ourselves treasure there that cannot be destroyed.

GOING OUT ON FAITH

You will recall Todd Beamer was one of the heroes on Flight 93 whose words, "Let's Roll" became the rallying cry for a nation going to war. However, the most poignant words Todd uttered that fateful day are often overlooked. They are buried in the transcript of the recording between Todd and the in-flight phone operator, Lisa Jefferson. During what must have been an excruciating moment, Todd said to Lisa, "It doesn't look like we're going to get out of this thing alive. We're going to have to go out on faith." I have been deeply impacted by those words. How insightful and intensely profound Todd was in his final observation.

Did he realize he was speaking for all of humanity? Who leaves earth "alive"? The statistics on death are fairly impressive. It's one for one. That's irrefutable. In the end, we all need to go out on faith. And that's why God sent His only Son to live among us, to take our sins upon Himself, to die on a cross, to be raised from the dead, to rule and reign forever and ever. Placing yourself in the will of God is the *only* way to "get out of this thing alive." It means taking a leap of faith.

Scripture tells us that "Now faith is being sure of what we hope for and certain of what we do not see" (Heb. 11:1).

Don't ask me to prove beyond a shadow of a doubt that there's a God. That's foolish and negates the purpose of faith. Some things have to be seen to be believed, and I say some things have to be believed to be seen. Were you really scared once? Prove it. Have you ever been in love? Prove it. Have you ever watched a sunset that took your breath away? Prove it. Some of us are in seemingly hopeless situations that squeeze the very life from us, and it doesn't look like we're going to make it out alive. And we're going to have to make it out by faith. No wishful thinking or "I hope so" mentality can substitute for unshakeable faith in a God who has promised to deliver us. "But hope that is seen is no hope at all. Who hopes for what he already has? But if we hope for what we do not yet have, we wait for it patiently" (Rom. 8:24–25).

FAITH IS THE THEME OF SCRIPTURE

What is faith? I like Webster's definition:

> faith (n) 1: confidence or trust in a person or a thing; a belief that is not based on proof; a belief in God or in the doctrines or teachings of religion; sticking to one's promise; oath, allegiance; faithful, steady 2: an allegiance or affection; loyal, constant, reliable, trusted, believed.

We talk about faith the size of a tiny mustard seed (Mark 4:31). We read about the spiritual heroes in the Hall of Faith

(Heb. 11). We cannot be saved without faith (John 3:36). We cannot live victoriously without faith (1 John 5:4). We cannot please God without faith (Heb. 11:6). We cannot pray without faith (James 1:6). We cannot have peace without faith (Rom. 5:1). We cannot have joy without faith (1 Peter 1:8). We are justified by faith, not by works (Gal. 2:16). We are to live by faith (Gal. 2:20). We are made righteous by faith (Rom. 10:4). Jesus dwells in our hearts by faith (Eph. 3:17). The Holy Spirit is received by faith (Gal. 3:2). Whatever is not of faith is sin (Rom. 14:23). Faith honors God. God honors faith.

Faith in a living God is essential in our ever-changing circumstances. Our faith wavers, but our God does *not*. Faith acts like a rudder that steers us forward in the midst of life's storms. Many people come and go from our lives. Friends have hurt me. I have hurt friends. My parents divorced after twenty-six years of marriage. Relationships have often been disappointing. My children do not always treat each other (or me) the way I had envisioned. Yet I've been a Christian over thirty years and can say without hesitation that Jesus has never let me down, never moved away, never pulled the rug out from under me, and never stabbed me in the back. He's never said, "Go away, clean up, and then come back. Get this straight, and then I'll see you." No, Jesus has been so faithful and kind, so merciful and tender.

FAITH REFUSES NEGATIVITY

A highly educated woman I know said to me, "I don't even believe Jesus existed." I thought to myself, *This has to be what the Bible refers to as the foolishness of the world.* What Ivy League school questions the existence of Plato and Aristotle? And yet, Jesus is up for debate? I didn't want to make her feel bad, but I thought, *Honey, even pagan historians agree He existed.* How sad that we've arrived in this postmodern Christian era where some have decided that He never even existed. The departure from biblical thought is not supposed to make us feel bad. Instead, it should make us mad. There are so many lies out there. Scripture reminds us that we live by faith and not by sight (2 Cor. 5:7). However, if we are not discerning, we can become addicted to negativity. We read *USA Today* and begin to believe the worst. We begin to feel depressed. Inferior. As if our faith isn't relevant. Have you been upset by CNN? Has your faith been affected by the headlines? A month after 9/11, my son, Jordan, asked, "Mom, are we going to die of anthrax?" (We live twenty-five miles outside of D.C.). And I dryly replied, "No, Jordan, but if you *don't* clean your room … !"

On February 13, 2003 the Director of Homeland Security raised the terror threat to Code Orange, the second highest level. While neighbors stormed Home Depot for duct tape and plastic sheeting, Frank and I boarded a flight from one target city (D.C.) to another (N.Y.). From the heights of the Rainbow Room atop Rockefeller Plaza we attended a fund-raiser for the homeless and watched a huge red heart light up the Empire State Building. Fear could have robbed me of this magical memory. We will not live foolishly, but neither will we live in fear. I will not be moved by headlines. I will not succumb to cowards. I will not be emotionally enslaved by the prince of this world because I serve the Prince of Peace. Instead of soaking up all the "bad news," we need to spend more time reading the "Good News," which "gives health to the bones" (Prov. 15:30).

FAITH MAKES A WAY

Faith makes a way where there seems to be no way. By the time I was in first grade, I was a full-fledged stutterer. Not quite as severe as Mel Tillis, but serious enough to break into cold sweats when I tried to convey a coherent sentence. My parents sent me to speech therapy for several years, and though I still stammer from time to time, that speech therapist would never have guessed that I would one day be a public speaker traveling throughout the country. God is not interested in our ability to impress Him as much as our availability to serve Him.

Don't despise the day of small beginnings. Don't stand in God's way. Satan will tell you every day what you are *not*. Tell him what and who you *are* in God's order of things. And remember we serve a God who "gives life to the dead and calls things that are *not* as though they *were*" (Rom. 4:17, emphasis added).

FAITH EXACTS A PRICE

I once heard a televangelist claim, "There is no need for suffering for those who belong to God." I wonder what version of the Bible that fellow is reading. "For to you it has been granted for Christ's sake, not only to believe in Him, but also to suffer for His sake" (Phil. 1:29 NASB). Is that *really* in the Bible? Suffer for His sake?

I want to be like Jesus, but I don't like pain. Isn't that interesting? I want to be like Jesus, but I don't want to be tested, stretched, pruned, or held over the refining fire. When Paul established the first church in Thessalonica, he paid dearly for his devotion and endured all kinds of persecution. In response, he wrote to his friends there, "No one should be shaken by these afflictions; for you yourselves know that we are appointed to this. For, in fact, we told you before when we were with you that we would suffer tribulation" (1 Thess. 3:3–4 NKJV). Appointed to suffer? *I'd like to change my appointment, please.* Why suffering? Because God can be seen in us through our suffering. Sometimes He allows pain and suffering to draw us (and those observing our trials) closer to Him.

In the Old Testament book of Daniel, three Hebrew teenagers willingly faced suffering in order to demonstrate the power of God to an entire pagan kingdom. After Daniel and his friends refused to bow before King Nebuchadnezzar's golden statue, the boys were sentenced to be burned to death inside the king's blazing furnace. Given one last chance to worship the idol and escape certain death, Daniel boldly confessed, "If we are thrown into the blazing furnace, the God we serve is able to save us from it" (Dan. 3:17). More amazing than that, Daniel conceded *even if* God chose not to save them, they would trust His ways and acknowledge Him as the only God.

The boys did escape. They emerged from the furnace unharmed. But that's not the end of the story. Eventually,

King Nebuchadnezzar himself became a convert to the God of Israel—in part because of what he had witnessed as a result of the boys' ordeal.

You see, suffering for God always leads to life. We experience a resurrection inside when we acknowledge God's ways are sovereign and just. The death of a child can bring people to the kingdom. Car wrecks where teenagers die bring people to the kingdom. Cancer brings people to the kingdom. The events of September 11 brought people to the kingdom. There are endless testimonies about how those who had parted ways with friends and family were moved to reconcile as a result of that horrendous day. The softening of hearts and rethinking of one's theology are wonderful potential results of tragic events.

I've had the privilege of attending various ceremonies for the National Day of Prayer. Some years ago, the audience heard from a young man named Josh from Columbine High School in Littleton, Colorado. He reported that the horrific shootings in 1999 resulted in a spiritual revival at Columbine. Some of the violence had erupted in a room called the greenhouse, which was adjacent to the science room. Now it's referred to as the greenhouse because people are being nurtured at the Spirit-filled meetings. It's still a real greenhouse, but aside from flowers, they're growing people. People of God. Josh stood in front of the bipartisan audience and asked with a daring tone, "*Who's* going to tell us not to pray in school? They wouldn't dare—not after what we've been through."

In her address at the 2003 National Prayer Breakfast, National Security Advisor Condoleeza Rice shared, "Only through struggle do we realize the depths of our resilience and understand that the hardest of blows can be survived and overcome. Too often when all is well, we slip into the false joy and satisfaction of the material and the complacent pride and faith in ourselves, yet it is through struggle that we find redemption and self knowledge, and in this sense it is a privilege to struggle, because it frees one from the idea that the human spirit is fragile, like a house of cards, or that human strength is fleeting."

The great theologian and author C. S. Lewis said, "In our blessings, God whispers, and in our suffering, he shouts." He calls pain God's "megaphone." I don't know about you, but when I'm in pain, God and I are tight. I talk to Him nonstop. I'm aware of His presence. I am looking for Him and I am inviting His presence into every room in my heart.

Pain will sometimes make us run, hide, or become bitter. When those unfortunate options become our daily choice, we continue in a slow downward path to an abyss that leaves us feeling lost and hopeless. Once there, we can't look beyond the suffering, the sickness, and death.

Good Friday must have seemed like the end to Jesus' followers. There were obvious reasons to give up, to lose hope, to wax cold. The Savior couldn't seem to save Himself. It was time to go home.

Three days later there was a resurrection.

What is *your* hopeless situation? What circumstance has *you* feeling like it's time to give up or give in? In the words of the colorful Christian sociologist, Tony Campolo, "It's Friday ... but Sunday's comin'!" There is a fellowship of the brokenhearted who are well acquainted with the shadows in the valley. Many learn to rejoice in the midst of their suffering because they have known a dimension of God that can never be experienced from the sunny side of the mountaintop.

LAYING DOWN OUR ISAAC

Abraham paid a tremendous price in order to receive God's promises. Not long after Abraham's son, the promised heir, had grown into a young boy, God asked Abraham to sacrifice Isaac upon an altar. He wanted Abraham to let go of the very one through whom all this blessing and promise was to come. So Abraham made the excruciating climb to the hillside altar, laid his precious boy down, and with trembling hands raised his knife. God's angel cried out to him, "Stop!" God told Abraham, "I know that you are willing. You have been tested and I know that you love me more than the promise." Each of us must ask ourselves if we prefer the gift or the Gift-giver.

We are not to cling to possessions, positions, or even people. Sometimes, we are stripped of these to reinforce the point. I attended Community Bible Study for six years and benefited greatly from the experience. As always, I became quite fond of a number of women I came to know there during those years. One special lady named Judy Cullen is an inspiring ambassador for Christ. She knows the Word, loves the Lord, and has a kind, gentle, and humble spirit. Before her beloved husband, Mel, died of a painful and aggressive cancer in his esophagus, he confided to Judy that the cancer was the best thing that had ever happened to him. It made him survey his life, count his blessings, and press closer to God than he had ever been before. Mel Cullen chose to treasure the Giftgiver (God Almighty) more than His gift of life on earth.

In my ministry, I'm coming across more and more people who are thanking God for their cancer. That response seems unnatural. These people embrace their suffering. They are able to embrace it because God accomplishes eternal things through it. Paul said he considered "everything a loss compared to the surpassing greatness of knowing Christ Jesus my Lord, for whose sake I have lost all things" (Phil. 3:8). What price is your heart willing to pay in exchange for the "surpassing greatness" of knowing Jesus more intimately? The leap of faith is costly, but the reward is priceless.

FROM FEAR TO FAITH

What happens if we refuse to pay the price? Ask Israel. The entire nation wandered around in circles, when all the while God wanted to bring them into the Promised Land. The typical journey from the Red Sea to Kadesh Barnea, which marked the entrance of the land flowing with milk and honey, was an eleven-day walk. Yet it took them forty years to arrive. How often we are like the Israelites, wandering for days on end, sometimes years, looking for the Promised Land—but wanting it on our own terms.

I want to remind you that you can go down your own path a long, long time. God will let you. Forty years is a long time for an eleven-day walk. In the same way, we may take five, ten, twenty, or even forty years doing things our own way when God would have preferred to provide us with specific directions. Without God's perspective, we may think we are farther along the road of life than we really are. I met a Canadian Ranger who tells the story of hikers who froze to death during a blizzard less than 100 yards from camp. In our spiritual journey, we must also remember that *close* to home isn't quite home.

I have spent forty-six years trying to navigate some paths that should have taken six months. Intellectually, I knew what I needed to do in order to be the best possible wife, mother, and friend I could be. I read the manuals. I listened to the experts. I knew the roadblocks and pitfalls. And yet, like Mr. Sinatra, I often did things "my way." If only I'd followed God's instructions from day one.

Proverbs 15:33 talks about the healthy role the fear of God can play in our lives when it comes to heeding His instructions: "The fear of the LORD teaches a man wisdom." Some women in my Bible study are repelled and offended by the notion of fearing God. In this generation, we have worked hard to hear "You've come a long way baby." We will not fear, cower, be slapped or bullied or emotionally eaten for lunch the way mother or grandma was. We look at the way mom was spoken to and say, "I'll never be spoken to that way." The women I teach each week are bright, multi-talented, and educated. They certainly refuse to take a step backward. And rightfully so. What misconceptions we have about "fearing the Lord!"

Yet, the fear of God is not a step backward. In the original Greek language, the root of this use of "fear" is linked to the word "awe." The fear of the Lord implies coming to terms with the awesome reality that He *is* God. That He created lightning. That He made fire. That tornadoes halt at His command. He is "the blessed and only Ruler, the King of kings and Lord of lords, who alone is immortal and who lives in unapproachable light, whom no one has seen or can see. To him be honor and might forever. Amen" (1 Tim. 6:15–16). In the Old Testament, nobody could see His face and live. Even the appearance of His celestial representatives, who are nowhere near His stature, caused everyone they visited to fall on their faces. Have you ever noticed that the very first words of the visiting angel are always, "Do not be afraid?" Doesn't that make you wonder what they look like?

When we "fear" the Creator, we are giving Him the respect He more than deserves from His creation. Proverbs 9:10 reminds us that "The fear of the Lord is the beginning of wisdom, and knowledge of the Holy One is understanding."

Conversely, we sometimes approach God so casually that we treat Him as if He were an investment broker. We want to consider our options when it comes to developing our spiritual portfolio. We hear God's instructions about where to work, whom to marry, where to live, etc. and we take that into account. Yet we consider His instructions one of many options. More like suggestions!

If we are honest with ourselves, we may be afraid of what God is going to ask us to do, so we choose to go our way instead. A healthy "fear," respect, and awe for God means we are more afraid of being *outside* of God's will, doing our own thing, than being safely *inside* it. How I long to be in the center of God's will. Like my young friend Kara, instead of being afraid of what comes next in His plan, I can have full assurance and confidence in His presence in the midst of it all. What a wonderful assurance ... what a wonderful place to rest.

CHAPTER SIX

LEAVING THE SANDS OF CERTAINTY

When we think of *overcoming*, we often think of physical maladies ranging from the inconveniences and nuisances related to the aging process to more serious examples of people who have survived horrible events and those born with disabilities. Joni Eareckson Tada, for example, became a quadriplegic in a diving accident. Yet she is a nationally recognized Christian speaker, author, and artist who learned how to create stunning paintings using a brush between her teeth. Christopher Reeve, well-known for his role as "Superman," has also done amazing things to advance his cause from a wheelchair.

When I flew to Sacramento to speak at a church retreat, I met an equally inspiring woman named Sue who greeted me in the airport and drove me to the retreat site. As we traveled together, this beautiful strawberry-blonde woman shared quite openly that she had recently undergone a double mastectomy. From her perspective, she explained, it was a "win/win" situation.

Thinking I had misunderstood, I inquired, "Win/win? Tell me about that."

"Well, if I get better," she began, "the glory will go to God. If I decline, people will pay more attention to my faith because of the sickness. My family has come closer to God. My husband's faith has deepened. And if I die, I'm going to be with Jesus. What is there to lose?"

We entered the church parking lot just about that time and I looked at Sue and told her, "*You* should be teaching this weekend, not me."

LAUGHING AT THE DAYS TO COME

We can all think of someone in our lives who is an overcomer. Maybe *you* are one. In some way, we are *all* overcomers who, like the godly woman in Proverbs 31, "can laugh at the days to come." Why does she laugh? Has she lost her mind? No—she laughs because she'll win in the end. She laughs because she knows the King is coming. She laughs because she realizes she will live forever.

We use the term "depression" so loosely these days. I'm not referring to serious clinical depression. For example, we're depressed because dinner burned or our new shoes got scuffed. And how many times do you hear kids say they're "so depressed" because their summer vacation is over or they missed their favorite TV show? It's important for us to realize that though we are unhappy at times, we can still have genuine joy. In the world's eyes, happiness depends on our circumstances. Remember Charlie Brown's song about happiness? *Crayons, skate keys, ice cream, singing a tune?* That's happiness. Happiness is finding a great parking spot at a crowded beach. It's when every piece of laundry is folded and put away. It's watching a favorite movie on TV with great hors d'oeuvres and the sound of rain on the windows. It's the Sunday *New York Times* with fresh bagels. *That's* happiness.

Allow me to return to the 1980s for a moment. That's the decade in which I devoted my life to the high calling of teaching English. Ahem. ... We find the root "hap" in the word happiness. In the Old Norse translation, hap is literally defined as "luck." We see it in words such as mishap, happenstance, and haphazard. All of these are tied to chance, circumstances, and the notion of change. Happiness is based on circumstance. It comes and goes.

In contrast, the Bible teaches us to be filled with joy in spite of unhappy, difficult, even painful circumstances. "In all our troubles my joy knows no bounds" (2 Cor. 7:4). Paul wrote those words while he was undergoing severe testing and trials on the mission field. From the same man, now penning a letter from inside a Roman prison, we read, "Rejoice in the Lord always. I will say it again: Rejoice!" (Phil. 4:4).

I chatted a long while with a woman named Barbara at a retreat in North Carolina. She has been through some pretty difficult trials regarding a rebellious teen. Parents of teens can relate to Barbara's familiar quandary. Teenagers test our very fiber. Abraham must have experienced Isaac's growing pains. Why do you think God asked Abraham to offer Isaac before he became a teenager? If they waited another year, it wouldn't have been such a sacrifice!

I have two teenagers and a twelve year old. I love them

all to death, and ironically, there are days they absolutely shorten my life expectancy. Paris is seventeen and driving everywhere. I'll never have to go out for milk and eggs again. Paris has informed me she was born for the stage and that she would like to study performing arts at UCLA. That's a long drive. Jordan debates anybody on anything, plays electronic games, and has been asking weird questions. "Ma—would you rather freeze to death or burn to death? How fast would a tyrannosaurus have to run to knock down the kitchen wall? How come we can have nuclear weapons and other countries can't? Who did Cain marry?" (Where's The Bible Answer Man when you need him?)

When Barbara told me her story, she concluded with sentiments similar to Paul's letter of joy to the Philippians. "But I have joy," she said with all sincerity. "I don't have joy because of the problem; I have joy in the midst of the problem. I'm not thanking God for this rebellious teenager right now. I'm thanking God for what He's *going* to do in my child's life." Barbara understood the promise, "that he who began a good work in you will carry it on to completion until the day of Christ Jesus" (Phil. 1:6). *That's* joy.

ATTITUDE ADJUSTMENT

The Bible says that Moses, after seeing the border of Canaan from afar, disqualified himself from entering the Promised Land because of his short temper. Likewise, many Israelites did not enter into the Promised Land because they were complainers. They were gripers. They were moaners.

God waited until all the disobedient people died—an entire generation—before He led the remaining Israelites into Canaan. The lesson to us? We must take inventory of our thoughts and actions and realize that God has no use for our bad attitudes. Stiff necks and hard hearts hurt others and ourselves. They keep us from experiencing all that He has for us.

On the south edge of Reston is a very nice Lutheran home for the elderly. It's actually a tall tower. I go there from time to time, and I sing some songs, tell some jokes, and play the guitar. I love sharing humor with the elderly. On my visits to the Hunter Woods retirement home, I've seen the Christian women in their 80s and 90s minister encouragement to the 60- and 70-year-old nonbelievers. They look the same age, but the difference between these two groups is less about numbers and more about their attitudes toward life. One is bitter and the other is better as a result of life's trials. One is hopeful and looking forward to seeing their loved ones again in heaven; one is waiting to die. One is quick to thank the children's choir from the church who visit; one resents the fact that nobody has thanked them in years. One feels like they have never had their day in the sun. And one is eager to enjoy every promise of heaven. Every trial in life will make us better or bitter. Our attitudes make all the difference.

Even the most elemental understanding of Genesis to Revelation reminds us that there is a wonderful, victorious, hopeful ending despite life's difficult circumstances. Life becomes a win/win situation, as God intended, when we realize we will arrive in Paradise as sure as the repentant thief on the cross who died alongside Jesus did. At my speaking engagements, I meet many wonderful people and hear so many stories. The brave and the broken. Victors and victims. Believers and doubters. Many of those stories linger in my head long after our encounter has passed.

I once met a mom whose eight- and ten-year-old boys were diagnosed with a rare cancer within six months of each other. The government authorized the EPA to dig under their house to see if their home is sitting on some sort of chemical site. I asked her, "How are you dealing with that? It seems unthinkable. Don't you feel like once was enough?" I'll never forget her answer.

She took a deep breath and explained, "I came to the point where I had to ask myself, 'What is the worst thing that could happen to Benjamin and Jacob?' The answer to that question would be death. And that will be bearable and even comforting only because if they leave here, they will immediately arrive in the presence of Jesus. There, they'll run around and play at His feet."

That's the *worst* that could happen? When I heard her say that, I loosened my grip and relaxed my knotted stomach. I took some oxygen into my frozen brain. I decided I would not let circumstances, nor the fear of death, overtake my attitude and rob me of my joy in Christ.

The whole idea of mind over matter is working its way into the public sector. However, it comes with a twist. My children attend school in Fairfax County—one of the largest school districts in the nation. At the one-year anniversary of 9/11 the administration sent home a booklet for each student's family in the school district entitled, "Helping America

Cope—A guide to help parents and children cope with the September 11, 2001 terrorist attacks and the aftermath." They encouraged parents to read the booklet together with their child and talk about their fears and issues.

Capri (my youngest) and I were flipping through this manual together when a subtitle caught my eye.

Q: *How can I teach my child to relax?*
A: *Use the Turtle Technique*

As I read through the paragraph, I recognized it as a sugar-coated version of transcendental meditation. The kids were to picture themselves creating a shell to hide inside their minds whenever they felt overwhelmed by fear and worry. *"Your child can create a shell by doing any of the following: putting his or her head down, going to a quiet corner or a separate room, or just closing his or her eyes. Once your child is in his or her shell, it is important to relax."* After describing deep-breathing and positive-imagining techniques, the manual continued to tell parents to instruct their children, *"Everyone is working very hard to keep you, your family, and your friends safe. People like the President and other leaders, the military, the police, the fire department, FBI, CIA, Coast Guard, etc. They are all working together to stop another attack."*

I put the booklet down, put my hands squarely on Capri's shoulders and told her that despite all of the increased security we enjoy, her government was not her bodyguard. The Fairfax County police make every effort to keep my children and the other members of our community safe, but they are not our bodyguards. Ultimately, Jesus is our bodyguard. *He* is doing everything possible to keep us safe in His hands.

Later that night, when I was alone, I continued reading Capri's booklet. My heart was so heavy. I was deeply saddened to be living in an age when my kids' schools were spelling out a Family Disaster Plan in case of bioterrorism or some other attack. I read on, *"Many disasters can occur without warning. Being prepared and knowing what to do if a disaster occurs can save you and your family's life. Create a family disaster plan. First, obtain information on how to prepare for disasters that may occur in your area* (hmmmm let's see ... The Pentagon bombing ... anthrax in the postal system ... the Beltway Sniper ... Hurricane Isabel). *Then hold a family meeting and develop your family's disaster plan. Make sure that everyone knows what to do, where to go, and who to call in the event a disaster occurs."*

That night as I prayed with tears in my eyes, God reminded me that those who follow Him have a meeting place, and it's not at the mailbox or the YMCA. That is incredibly comforting. My family will not remain separated because of a dirty bomb or the smallpox virus or a meteor. These are unsettling days. But in the midst of all of it, we look forward to a glorious reunion one day in heaven. The Lofaro family *does* have a meeting place. It's heaven's front gate. We will meet there and we will celebrate and sing of God's faithfulness. In the face of such uncertainty, the words Todd Beamer expressed on the in-flight phone are even more telling. "We're not going to make it out of here alive ... we're going to have to go out on faith."

While writing this book, I received the news that a spiritual giant, Dr. Bill Bright, entered glory. He was the founder and longtime president of Campus Crusade for Christ, author of *The Four Spiritual Laws*, and champion of *The Jesus Film*. I'd *love* to get a glimpse of *that* homecoming party! One night when my friend Patsy and I were talking, she reminded me that God created our bodies with expiration dates. We start to leave this world from the moment we enter it. How wise is the believer who doesn't get too comfortable here.

C. S. Lewis once remarked, "If you read history you will find that the Christians who did most for the present world were just those who thought most of the next. The Apostles themselves, who set on foot the conversion of the Roman Empire, the great men who built up the Middle Ages, the English Evangelicals who abolished the Slave Trade, all left their mark on Earth, precisely because their minds were occupied with Heaven. It is since Christians have largely ceased to think of the other world that they have become so ineffective in this one. Aim at Heaven and you will get Earth 'thrown in'—aim at Earth and you will get neither."[6]

God uses trials and troubles to help us to yearn for glory. "For instance, we know that when these bodies of ours are taken down like tents and folded away, they will be replaced by resurrection bodies in heaven—God-made, not hand-made—and we'll never have to relocate our 'tents' again. Sometimes we can hardly wait to move—and so we cry out in frustration. Compared to what's coming, living conditions around here seem like a stopover in an unfurnished shack, and we're tired of it! We've been given a glimpse of the real thing, our true home, our resurrection bodies!" (2 Cor.

5:1–4 MSG). Our attitude should be that of Pope John Paul II, who recently declared, "My bags are packed and I'm ready to go." I don't mean a pie-in-the-sky mentality, but instead a willingness to concede that this is not our home. For me, the journey thus far has been more than wonderful. But life *is* a journey with a final destination that is *truly* out of this world.

RIVERS OF IMPOSSIBILITY

The book of Joshua is a historical account of how an entire generation became overcomers.

> After the death of Moses the servant of the LORD, the LORD said to Joshua son of Nun, Moses' aide: "Moses my servant is dead. Now then, you and all these people, get ready to cross the Jordan River into the land I am about to give to them—to the Israelites. I will give you every place where you set your foot, as I promised Moses." (Josh. 1:1–3)

Before the remaining Israelites could enter the Promised Land, they had to forge a river of impossibility. The Jordan River literally stood in the way between them and all that God had waiting for them. They questioned God's logic. *Why did He take us this way?* They questioned His timing. As the snow from the Lebanon Mountains melted, freezing cold water had flooded the river. *Why do we have to cross this river, at flood stage no less?*

More than anything else, our attitude regarding life's challenges reveals what we deeply believe about God's faithfulness. Our own river of impossibility is anything that stands in the way of our receiving God's promises. It can be a particular habit, sin, or fear. Yet God says to us, "You and I are going to get over to the other side of this together. I don't want you to miss out on the blessings I have planned for you. I am concerned about the things that are dividing your attention and distracting you."

What is your river of impossibility today? What is it about your future that has you afraid to leave the shores of security? What or who are you afraid to leave behind? In order to pursue what God has for you tomorrow you may have to leave something, someplace, or someone behind today.

Two Choices

Israel had two choices. Either they could stay behind on the dry riverbank of the Jordan River where they had camped for three days. Or they could take a leap of faith.

> Early in the morning Joshua and all the Israelites set out from Shittim and went to the Jordan, where they camped before crossing over. After three days the officers went throughout the camp, giving orders to the people: "When you see the ark of the covenant of the LORD your God, and the priests, who are

Levites, carrying it, you are to move out from your positions and follow it. Then you will know which way to go, *since you have never been this way before.*" (Josh. 3:1–4 emphasis added)

Can you relate to the Israelites' situation? "God, I haven't been this way before. I haven't had a child break my heart like this. I haven't experienced a life-threatening illness. I haven't had a parent with Alzheimer's before. No one in my family has ever divorced before. I've never been tempted in this situation before. I haven't had my best friend stab me in the back. I've never been out of work. Lord, I haven't been this way before!"

God assured Joshua, "You will know which way to go" (v. 4). When our footsteps falter as we contemplate the deep waters of our river of impossibility, God says, "Follow me. Then you will know which way to go. You'll know how to act and what to say in order to overcome."

On one side of the Jordan River, Israel camped on its riverbanks. On the other side of the river, a land flowing with milk and honey awaited them. In order to enter their inheritance they would have to make a choice. Unbelief says, "We can't cross over. Let's go back to where it's safe." Faith says, "Let's go forward. God will make a way." There weren't any bridges, mind you. No boats. God was about to take them to a new dimension of faith. A new level of trust. But they had to make a choice.

TWO KINDS OF CHRISTIANS

The Christian that is an overcomer.
The Christian that is being overcome.

The Christian that is living in victory.
The Christian that is living in defeat.

The Christian that is full of joy.
The Christian that has little or no joy.

The Christian that has a testimony.
The Christian that has a complaint.

Despite our deep and abiding love for God, sometimes life's heartaches cloud our vision of Him. Do you feel He has become a far off God who is granting abundant life to others but certainly not to you? You may wonder if Jesus has any idea what you're going through. In frustration, you may have raised your voice and fist toward heaven crying, "Jesus, you say I can be an overcomer, but what do *you* know about my pain?" How easily we forget. Actually, Jesus knew all about pain and suffering.

Jesus, do you know what it's like to be physically afflicted?
I hung on a cross, and every time I tried to lift myself for a breath, I felt the nails drive deeper into my flesh. My lungs were crippled, and I could hardly gasp.

Jesus, do you know what it's like to grow up in a single family home?
My earthly father died young. My mother struggled as a widow. I know what it's like to be different from other families.

Jesus, do you know what it's like to be abused?
The soldiers pressed thorns deep into my forehead and laughed as they did it. As I hung on the cross dying, they gambled for my clothing at my feet.

Jesus, do you know what it's like to be sexually abused?
I was fully naked as scoffers passed and scorned my name, caring nothing for my agony.

Jesus, do you know what it's like to be betrayed by friends?
My friends couldn't even stay with me for an hour in the garden the night I was betrayed. When I needed them most, my closest companions denied they even knew me.

Jesus, do you know what it's like to be scared to take that step of faith?
I prayed for the Lord to let me pass through the terrible death that awaited me. I was so distraught that my sweat fell to the ground like droplets of blood.

Jesus, do you know what it's like to be human?
Yes, I know. That's exactly why I came.

DON'T LINGER TOO LONG

Some people stand on the riverbanks of impossibility and decide to bide their time. They may refuse to go forward. They may decide to wait for the floods to recede. For the wind to change. For the week to pass. Lingering too long in the quagmire of doubt and indecision can prove disastrous.

If you've ever watched circus performers dangle upside down from the trapeze, swinging back and forth waiting for the perfect sweep of momentum to wing them to the next trapeze, you have a mental image of where many people are in their pursuit of God. One of the most uncertain places to be in our spiritual lives is "between trapezes"—hovering between the known and the unknown. No one is standing still, you know. Some of us are swinging back into the past—past problems, past habits. We even like looking over our shoulder at past victories, satisfied to admire all we once did for the Lord. We are waiting for things to be just right before we release our grip and take that leap. We even ask other people to give us their opinion because we say we want to be sure that we're following God's voice and not our own. We may stall for more time reading lots of books and tapes before we'll take the leap. A businessman asked his pastor to pray for him regarding a decision he had to make. "I just don't know what to do. Pray for me to have certainty," the man said. The pastor smiled and replied, "I won't pray for you to have certainty. But I will pray for you to have faith." The perfect boat, plane, train, or trapeze rarely comes along. However, we can count on the absolute certainty that God is there to catch us. That's why it's called a leap *of faith*.

PART
THREE

CHAPTER SEVEN

WHAT NOW?

The season finale of the overblown talent show *American Idol* captured the attention of 25.3 million viewers in 2003, topped only by the 25.5 million who watched the season finale of the young adult sitcom, *Friends*. According to the industry ratings, the final episode of the dating reality show *The Bachelor* turned in a "disappointing" mere 15 million viewers. That's called a "following" any way you look at it. I think we can safely conclude that America is watching television with extremely compromised standards.

Sadly, many people base their understanding of relationships on the story line of popular sitcoms or "reality" programs (which ironically distort reality more than they portray it). The public is fascinated by the love lives of movie stars. Christians must not turn to the gossip column or the cable channel to find truth. We know better. We should adjust our habits and choices within a framework that causes us to be in God's will. So, where *do* we forge our opinions? For many of us, the answer to that question is highly subjective, and it may not be any different from the world's response. It's amazing how much "stuff" we will allow into our minds. Are you feeding your mind on biblical truth or are you trying to navigate life with junk food and a remote control? Let's be very careful. The days hold all sorts of darkness.

> But mark this: There will be terrible times in the last days. People will be lovers of themselves, lovers of money, boastful, proud, abusive, disobedient to their parents, ungrateful, unholy, without love, unforgiving, slanderous, without self-control, brutal, not lovers of the good, treacherous, rash, conceited, lovers of pleasure rather than lovers of God—having a form of godliness but denying its power. Have nothing to do with them. They are the kind who worm their way into homes and gain control over weak-willed women, who are loaded down with sins and are swayed by all kinds of evil desires, always learning but never able to acknowledge the truth. (2 Tim. 3:1–7)

Does that sound a little bit like modern-day America? And who might be entering our houses? Might it be seductive or violent television, books, or movies? These destructive images don't force their way into our homes. Although we would certainly never welcome a promiscuous or violent intruder into our homes, sadly, we often hold the door open for unedifying media images that prance right in through televisions, computers, stereos, and magazines. We don't realize how worldly influences stick to our souls with oppressive heaviness until we try to free ourselves. Have you ever tried to have a family prayer time after a questionable movie? Have you tried reading the Bible right after reading a magazine that features a lot of skin? Have you tried to glorify God after playing a video game that glorifies violence? I am continually challenged on a personal level in all of these things. I have walked out of movie theaters, novelty shops, and t-shirt stores, while informing the proprietor why I will not support them with my finances. Jesus said, "If you hold to my teaching, you are really my disciples. Then you will know the truth, and the truth will set you free" (John 8:31–32).

We're living in a relativistic age where truth is up for grabs. People feel quite confident saying things like, "Your truth is not my truth, and my truth is not your truth. And really, what is truth anyway and who's to say one is superior to another?" No one wants to be accused of being intolerant. Jesus, on the other hand, makes a clearly exclusive claim to truth. "I am the way and the truth and the life. No one comes to the Father except through me" (John 14:6). All that Jesus said and did is truth. You either believe Jesus or you don't. He was too radical, controversial, and shocking for any of us to remain neutral about Him. You either buy it or you don't. You're either in or you're out. Straddling the fence in regard to truth, while socially chic, is neither attractive nor fitting for a Capital "C" Christian.

Are we embarrassed to share our Christian views? Do

we find ourselves shrinking back at the water cooler at work when "religion" comes up? Maybe you grow quiet because you haven't studied seriously enough, or maybe you're concerned about what others will think of you. Jesus clearly warned of the consequences of such behavior. "If anyone is ashamed of me and my words, the Son of Man will be ashamed of him when he comes in his glory and in the glory of the Father and of the holy angels" (Luke 9:26).

Listen closely to what the Bible has to say about our knowledge of His Word. "But as for you, continue in what you have learned and have become convinced of, because you know those from whom you learned it, and how from infancy you have known the holy Scriptures, which are able to make you wise for salvation through faith in Christ Jesus. All Scripture is God-breathed and is useful for teaching, rebuking, correcting and training in righteousness, so that the man of God may be thoroughly equipped for every good work" (2 Tim. 3:14–17). I know people who have the latest bestsellers on their nightstand, but they don't know if they're coming or going. They have read the latest seven-step book, but they cannot defeat a deadly habit. They have mastered their golf or tennis swing, but not their propensity to gossip. Apart from God and an understanding of His reign over all things seen and unseen, there will never be knowledge of truth. Apart from God, there is no truth.

Why are people breaking down? Why are the sales of drugs (legal and illegal) breaking records? Why are half of the marriages not making it? Why do people end up hating the children they gave birth to, and vice versa? Why do families stop talking for years? I believe we are breaking down as individuals and as a society because we have ignored God. Oh, we say "God bless America" and we fill churches, but very few who choose fellowship mature to the point of choosing lordship. A friend who runs a Bible school in Tanzania likes to say, "Jesus is Lord of all—or not at all." Severe? I think not. Slowly but steadily, the moral and spiritual fiber of this country is unraveling. Oh, how we need a Savior! He mends us and gives us hope. We cannot take a Mercedes to a bicycle repair shop and expect to receive expert advice and care. They won't even have the right parts! In the same way, we can't take a broken human to a motivational guru and expect him to give us the answers to make us whole again. As Christians, we must go to the Word of God when we are in search of truth. It's an unchanging, timeless, reliable, eternal truth. His name is Jesus.

> In the beginning was the Word, and the Word was with God, and the Word was God. He was with God in the beginning. Through him all things were made; without him nothing was made that has been made. In him was life, and that life was the light of men. (John 1:1–4)

CAUGHT OFF GUARD

"If you'd made me stay home and study instead of letting me go to soccer practice, then this wouldn't have happened, you know!" My youngest child once said this as she cleverly attempted to explain why she didn't do too well on a math test. Ever notice how there is a perfectly reasonable explanation for our mistakes whenever we can place blame on someone else? Sometimes, I offer similarly lame excuses to God. "If You had only ..."

When we have not prepared ourselves spiritually in advance of a crisis situation, we tend to react with similar childish predictability. We become flustered and angry with God, friends, family, coworkers, neighbors, and ultimately with ourselves when we are caught unprepared for one of life's "tests." The concept of personal responsibility is very unpopular. We blame other people, but we don't want to be blamed. *Well, you don't understand. I'm like this because of my mother. You should see my family, and that would explain me. You should have been around when my father lost his temper.* There is definite truth to the fact that our experiences in life deeply affect the health of our hearts—both physically and emotionally. But how long are we willing to remain resentful, sick, and broken? Let the Word of God begin to heal you and fortify your weak places so when the next test comes along you will be stronger and better prepared. Scripture tells us that "Christ loved the church and gave himself up for her to make her holy, cleansing her by the washing with water through the word, and to present her to himself as a radiant church, without stain or wrinkle or any other blemish, but holy and blameless" (Eph. 5:25–27).

The Bible says to be prepared with God's Word "in season" and "out of season" according to 2 Timothy 4:2. That means we can't take time off when we don't feel particularly inspired to read God's Word. That's when self-discipline kicks in. It is our responsibility to make the choice to be prepared to live out genuine Christianity whether or not we "feel like it."

MORE THAN A CASSEROLE

Tragically, my sister's neighbor committed suicide. The next time I visited Michelle, my heart just broke when I saw the teenage boy who found his father's body in the garage. The boy was out in the street mechanically bouncing a basketball and shooting. He looked numb and expressionless. Bouncing, bouncing, shooting, bouncing and shooting.

I said to my sister, "Have you been over there to visit?"

"Oh, no," she replied. "I took a casserole when it first happened, but I haven't been back. I wouldn't know what to say."

Few of us are entirely comfortable with tragedy, but we need to bring more than a casserole to the door of a home, a hospital, a funeral parlor, or a prison cell. As Christians, we can enter any of these difficult places with so much more than a glib "good luck" and well-intentioned "hang in there." In fact, when we *know* Jesus, we have an abundance of gifts to bring to those who are hurting. A good, hard listen—a shoulder to cry on—a word of life in the midst of death. Most of all, we can extend the hope and love of Jesus, the God of all comfort. "Praise be to the God and Father of our Lord Jesus Christ, the Father of compassion and the God of all comfort, who comforts us in all our troubles, so that we can comfort those in any trouble with the comfort we ourselves have received from God" (2 Cor. 1:3–4). As believers we are called to bring the "bread of life" along with the casserole. God wants all of us to grow in knowledge and wisdom of His ways. They are higher than ours, but thanks to the cross, they are fully within reach.

If I had a fire hose and your house was on fire, I wouldn't politely wait for the right moment to stop over. If I had the cure to a terminal disease, why wouldn't I share it so that lives could be spared? We haven't mentioned Jesus because we don't want to *offend* anyone? No wonder so many families are steeped in crisis. The Christian neighbors didn't say anything. If you know of a way people can live forever, and how people can have joy and peace and abundant life, and you don't tell anybody, that choice is not polite—it's tragic.

Just when did we become so fearful? In the old neighborhood, the aunts used to call each other when there was a great sale at the market. Some people call when they need a signature. Telemarketers call every day—*gotta get that zapper.* There's lots of information out there, and so much of it leads nowhere. What holds us back from wanting to tell people about the truth? The Bible exhorts us to, "Always be prepared to give an answer to everyone who asks you to give the reason for the hope that you have" (1 Peter 3:15).

I was very moved by a story I heard about a typical Sunday evening service in a very small church. The pastor was getting ready to begin the service, the elders were seated and the teenagers were giggling and passing notes—especially two boys seated in the small balcony. Seemingly ignoring their antics, the pastor announced he had a special pulpit guest with him that night—a man he had known for many years. An elderly man left his seat on the front row and made his way to the pulpit.

The old man began his sermon by telling a story about a father, his fifteen-year-old son, and his son's friend who went sailing together one evening off the northern California coast. The father was a pastor and also a proficient sailor. However, that night's horrendous storm would soon put his maritime skills to the ultimate test in more ways than one. After he bailed water out of the hull for over two hours during the violent rain, the sailboat finally capsized.

All three tumbled into the darkness of the raging sea. The father was closest to the overturned sailboat and struggled to secure a lifeline to a buoy. Straining to see the two boys during the brief flashes of lightning, he was horrified to realize that the two boys were succumbing to the unrelenting waves, but they were too far apart to reach both with the one lifeline.

As the fierce waves tossed their fragile bodies about, the father faced a terrible dilemma. He knew that his son was a Christian, and that if he died that night, he would immediately be in the presence of Jesus. Yet his son's best friend did not have the same hope. Not only did the boy not believe— he was quite verbal about his hatred and repulsion by all things religious. The father could not bear for that boy to face eternity apart from Jesus. So the moment the lightning lit the sky, with his body shaking and his heart breaking, the father looked in his son's direction and screamed out, "I love you, Son! I love you!" He then threw the lifeline out to his son's friend.

By this time, the congregation was riveted to the old man's story, including the two teens in the back. The man concluded his message by drawing a parallel between the story and God's sacrificial love for us that permitted His Son to die so that we could live. "God has thrown us a lifeline. He allowed his sweet Son to die so that we could live." It was a powerful moment and the congregation was deeply moved. After the service, the two boys quickly walked to the front pew and approached the old man. "That's a really good story, mister, but it's not very realistic. The man didn't even know if his son's friend was ever going to become a Christian." To which the old gentleman replied, "You're right—it's not very logical or realistic. Again, what an amazing illustration of God's love for us. But it *is* a true story. In fact, it's *my* story. You see, I was that father, and your pastor was my son's friend."

There is a costly lifeline of love that has been tossed out to you. When you grab hold of Jesus, you will be saved. Open your arms. Open your heart. Open your mind so that it can be renewed—not with the psychobabble being thrust at you each day—but with the life-changing Word of God which is reliable and true. Do you know Jesus? Or have you settled for knowing *about* Jesus? What a vast difference. Jesus is the one true God. Accept no substitutes.

If you have indeed had the salvation experience, then you must be prepared to pass the lifeline along so that others can find the safe haven you have enjoyed. Jesus is good news—tell people. Jesus is the bread of life—feed people. Jesus is a spring of living water that will never run dry—lead others to the well. Jesus is the banquet that brings all the bounty and beauty we dream of—invite people. "It's news I'm most proud to proclaim, this extraordinary Message of God's powerful plan to rescue everyone who trusts him" (Rom. 1:16 MSG).

BE SET APART

Joshua told the people, "Consecrate yourselves, for tomorrow the LORD will do amazing things among you." Joshua said to the priests, "Take up the ark of the covenant and pass on ahead of the people." So they took it up and went ahead of them. And the LORD said to Joshua, "Today I will begin to exalt you in the eyes of all Israel, so they may know that I am with you as I was with Moses. Tell the priests who carry the ark of the covenant: 'When you reach the edge of the Jordan's waters, go and stand in the river.'" (Josh. 3:5–8)

The Hebrews were tired. They'd been traveling forty years. The last thing they wanted to do was encounter yet another hurdle on their way home. However, God knew His people needed to step back, take some time, and prepare for this final leg of the journey—perhaps their most difficult trek yet. In order to overcome life's challenges, we have to discipline ourselves along the same lines. When the job is lost, when the loved one dies, when the body fails, whenever life's storms blow our way with hurricane force, let's be prepared in our faith instead of being easily thrown off balance.

The most important way Israel prepared to cross the Jordan River was to "consecrate" themselves. Holiness reminded the people of God that every step along this momentous journey had to be done God's way. They could have done it their way—camping out, building boats, and getting across the river in due time. However, in order for them to experience what God had in mind, they had to do things His way.

The Israelites were preparing to enter into the Promised Land—which was presently occupied by pagan people. However, these pagans would soon witness the power of God among this strange band of nomads, two million strong. Joshua said in 3:10, "By this you shall know that the living God is among you, and that he will assuredly dispossess from before you the Canaanites, the Hittites, the Hivites, the Perizzites, the Girgashites, the New Jerseyites, and the ter-mites." (NASB paraphrased. Sorry, Jersey.)

Being "set apart" is not the same as being separatist. The term "consecrate" used in Joshua 3:5 has to do with being set apart for God's purposes. Any separation that takes place must be one that pulls us away from danger and closer to God's safety. Separating ourselves from sin is important because it requires change. We must be resolute about not acting like self-willed, disobedient children. We have a responsibility to pursue the very character of God in our everyday lives. The Bible says, "For we know that our old self was crucified with him so that the body of sin might be done away with, that we should no longer be slaves to sin" (Rom. 6:6).

Moving "south" to the land of Robert E. Lee was a major cultural adjustment. New York was all we had known. In our new "southern" life, I was busy presiding over the Parent Teacher Fellowship (PTF), a Christian PTA, Frank was working for a ministry, and all three kids were in Christian schools. We had joined a Christian church surrounded by Christian friends. We were immersing ourselves in a Christian subculture, and, in my opinion, we were dangerously close to a separatist form of Christianity. It bothered me because I believe it's important to be salt and light instead of spending all our time and energy with like-minded people. Jesus didn't wait for the culture to come to hear Him at the temple. He went out to the street, the hillside, the well, the sea, the dirt road, the homes. I want to do the same.

However, genuine Christians *must* be set apart since we are to emulate a holy God. In our pursuit of holiness, we must be sure not to be exclusionary or aloof from non-Christians. If we purport to be "holier than thou," we're not going to winsomely affect anybody for Christ. Jesus didn't win converts by being divisive and derogatory. He won converts by offering to do lunch, go fishing, and attend parties.

In his book, *What's So Amazing About Grace?*, Philip Yancey tells a story about a prostitute in her thirties who involved her teenage daughter in prostitution. He couldn't believe this was going on and wanted to help her in some way. One day, when he saw her on the street, he said what many of us might have offered to someone in a similar scenario. "Have you considered going to a church for help?" he asked. Her response was telling. "Going to a church?" she said with resolute sadness. "Why would I go to a church? I feel bad enough about myself already."

Who is welcome in our churches? Would the prostitute and her daughter feel welcome? Mother Teresa said that if we're busy judging people, we cannot love them. People crave fellowship, and they'll look for love and acceptance wherever they can. But do they readily discover it in our houses of worship?

Jesus never said, "Clean up, smell good, dress right, and quit that habit! *Then* you can come to Me." He said, "It is not the healthy who need a doctor, but the sick. I have not come to call the righteous, but sinners" (Mark 2:17). Why are we constantly trying to get people to a place where we're comfortable with them? We grow indignant if someone else dares to intrude upon our holy huddles. We've all observed the unfortunate souls who are upset about newcomers. They'll say, "Hey, wait a minute. This is *our* church circle. You don't belong." I've met people who have left Bible studies, home groups, and churches because of growth in attendance. Imagine that.

There are some churches where one has to be part of the inner circle in order to feel at home. I call groups like these the "chosen frozen." The Church of the Holy Dress Code. The Church of the Abundant Casserole. I want to say to these folks, "If the joy of the Lord is your strength ... please inform your face." The joy God gives is irrepressible and irresistible. I pray that the people who don't look like us or smell like us or talk like us or walk like us are welcome to be wherever we are. However, I'm afraid that some churches have turned into country clubs and social clubs, when we were intended to be hospitals. Why hospitals? Because we are all in need of the Great Physician. We're all broken. We're all sinners.

GOD'S STANDARD OF HOLINESS

The sooner we recognize that we're all sinners, the better. When we realize that we could never measure up to a holy God's standards on our own, we're on our way to healing. We can finally be genuine. Remove the mask. Get some help. Begin to confess. We must understand that we're helpless and hopeless without the restoration that God can bring through His Son, Jesus Christ.

Amy Carmichael, a dynamic missionary to India who lived in the nineteenth century, understood restoration and hope:

"If I belittle those who I'm called to serve, if I talk about their weak points in contrast perhaps with what I think of as my strong points, if I adopt a superior attitude, then I know nothing of Calvary love. If I take offense easily, if I am content to continue in cold unfriendliness, though friendship is possible, then I know nothing of Calvary love. If I feel bitterly toward those who condemn me, as it seems unjustly, forgetting that *if they knew me as I know myself, they would condemn me even more*, then I know nothing of Calvary love" [7] (emphasis added).

Sheila Walsh went from being the co-host of *The 700 Club* to a psychiatric hospital where she was diagnosed with severe clinical depression. She is now a devoted wife and mom, not to mention a gifted author and speaker with Women of Faith. She is a powerful testimony of God's grace. She has shared the story of coming off the air one day from the *700 Club* set and confiding in some colleagues that she was going to sign herself into a psychiatric ward later that afternoon. One of her associates at the station cautioned her in the parking lot, "Sheila, you'll never work again. Don't do it." This person reminded her about all the media coverage that could ensue. Later, after she left her celebrated career, another person with whom she had candidly shared her struggles with depression conveyed disappointment with Sheila. *How could a Christian take anti-depressants?* Although she was deeply hurt by the comments, Sheila wisely responded, "I'm so sorry you're disappointed, but if you knew everything about me, then you would be *really* disappointed."

When we are at the end of ourselves, there is nothing left to lose, is there? I'm learning about the freedom and comfort of knowing that I can never meet God's standards on my own. I cannot measure up apart from Him. When we are willing to recognize just how far we fall short, then we can say to Jesus, "Please, help me."

TRUST AND OBEY

Remind the people to be subject to rulers
and authorities, to be obedient, to be ready to

do what is good, to slander no one, to be peace-
able and considerate, and to show true humil-
ity toward all men. (Titus 3:1–2)

I like the word "obedience" as it pertains to my children,
but how do *you* like the word "obedience?" Personally, I have
a lot of problems with it insofar as it concerns *me*. My husband reminds me from time to time that I have certain issues
with authority. He says I don't think certain rules are meant
for me—like a thirty mile-an-hour speed limit.

Even so, obedience is important. My children should obey
me. Things work out well for them when they do. I have
years of wisdom and authority that they don't, and I have
their well-being in mind. I see things they do not see. I have
a perspective of the big picture. I can sense danger around the
bend. As a heavenly Father, God sees what we lack the maturity to see. He knows what we don't know, so He asks us to
trust and obey Him. He definitely has the big picture. He sees
what's around the bend. God wants us to humble ourselves
and obey and to hold His hand at life's intersections. We also
need to ask for His help so that we can make good choices,
accept His forgiveness, and be made whole. "'Come now, let
us reason together,' says the LORD. 'Though your sins are like
scarlet, they shall be as white as snow; though they are red as
crimson, they shall be like wool'" (Isa. 1:18).

Am I perfect? Of course not. No one is perfect. Am I growing to be more and more like Jesus? I pray so. Am I a better
ambassador for Christ than I was five years ago? One year
ago? By God's grace, the answer is yes. Do I hope to show

improvement six months from now? Most definitely. In the words of an old Baptist preacher, *"We ain't what we wanna be— but thank God we ain't what we used to be!"* Amen to that.

CHAPTER EIGHT

GOING PUBLIC

I've always felt I could be a great Christian if it were not for other people. I've also insisted I could be a great wife if it weren't for Frank! I have come to learn the concept is not original to me. In fact, the first monks were called "hermits," a term derived from a Greek word meaning "to desert." They deserted community life in favor of a solitary existence. In fact, the most unusual examples of first-century monks were called Pillar People who literally lived on top of stone pillars. Following the lead of a monk named Simeon, who lived for more than thirty years atop a sixty-foot stone pillar, the Pillar People believed that the best way to avoid sin was to avoid people.

People came from nearby towns to gawk at the strange sight. The monks couldn't communicate with anyone down below because of their vows of silence. They couldn't get into arguments. They couldn't get offended. They couldn't get their feelings hurt if someone didn't agree with them. These Pillar People were not living with people, but they were also not living in reality. If we want to live a meaningful life, we have to reckon with the ups and downs of interacting with others.

We will certainly meet resistance when we attempt to live wholeheartedly for Jesus. Sometimes the resistance is blatant spiritual warfare. And sometimes it is the result of the human condition. We are capable of much discord. You will meet resistance serving as a Christian on the public school board. If you want to have trouble with people, join a church committee. If you want to doubt your salvation, run the committee! And Satan? Satan won't go looking for you in a smoke-filled nightclub. He'll come straight to your kitchen or the church meeting room. The Bible refers to him as the "accuser of the brethren" whose job it is to thwart any and all of your efforts to serve Jesus. You will not have any more trouble with the devil when you die. And if he doesn't bother you much, you might be half-dead already.

English preacher, Henry Jowett, once observed, "It is possible to evade a multitude of sorrows through the cultivation of an insignificant life. Indeed, if a person's ambition is to avoid the troubles of life, the recipe is simple: Shed your ambitions in every direction, cut the wings of every soaring purpose, and seek a life with the fewest contacts and relations. If you want to get through life with the smallest trouble, you must reduce yourself to the smallest compass. Tiny souls can dodge through life; bigger souls are blocked on every side. As soon as a person begins to enlarge his or her life, resistances are multiplied. Let a person remove petty selfish purposes and enthrone Christ, and suffering will be increased on every side."

When we prepare ourselves with God's Word, when we decide to passionately pursue holiness and set ourselves and our families apart, we will begin to change. And when we begin to change, it will not go unnoticed. We will encounter resistance.

If your lifestyle, thoughts, and behavior are *no* different from when you were a nonbeliever, you need to take personal inventory. Conversion to Christ results in change. He's in the miracle business and when we give Him access to our control panel, that's exactly what we are—we're miracles! The Bible says we are a royal priesthood. A chosen people. We have a sense of our calling and a sense of duty. Yet, we must be willing to face opposition because the mission runs counterculture.

We often refer to those who diverge from mainstream humanity as going against the flow, but the Israelites were literally going against the flow when they stepped out on faith and into the Jordan River. A giant wall of freezing water suddenly swirled around their feet and threatened to drown them or give them hypothermia. Talk about meeting resistance!

> See, the ark of the covenant of the Lord of all the earth will go into the Jordan ahead of you. Now then, choose twelve men from the tribes of Israel, one from each tribe. And as soon as the priests who carry the ark of the LORD—the Lord of all the earth—set foot in the Jordan, its waters flowing downstream will be cut off and stand up in a heap. (Josh. 3:11–13)

In times of national prosperity and great spiritual freedom, we have lost sight of the concept and understanding of the greatest form of resistance—religious persecution. We've softened our understanding of how tough it is to be a "sold out" Christian. We feel persecuted when someone questions our bumper sticker or leaves us out of the next luncheon. However, we haven't run across people whose teeth have been punched out by the authorities because they were meeting for Bible study.

That disclaimer aside, 2 Timothy 3:12 reminds us, "In fact, everyone who wants to live a godly life will be persecuted." In America, we may lose jobs because of our faith. Mates may walk out because of our devotion. If we're out on the spiritual battlefield answering to Jesus Christ and His commands, we're likely being shot at on a daily basis no matter what part of the world we live in.

Many men and women with varied duties contributed to carrying out the mission during the war with Iraq. They did not necessarily have to be on the front lines to fulfill their duty. If you remember, soldiers from the maintenance crews were some of the first P.O.W.s. We can't go through our entire Christian experience hanging back from the front lines. If we are going public with our faith, we will face the gates of hell. We will encounter resistance. We will catch flak.

Ten years of public school teaching resulted in a deep aversion to participating in assisting my children with homework. I choose not to get involved. When they ask for help, I tell them, "I did fifth grade. I did very well. I'm done with fifth grade. Good luck in fifth grade." My husband, on the other hand, is like a drill sergeant. He wanted our first grader to do rough drafts. "Frank, go easy on them," I tell him. When my son got a C, Frank promptly gave him the "You'll be in the street ... you'll be homeless if you fail in school" speech.

Paris was in honors English one year in high school with a wildly liberal teacher. The teacher assigned books that didn't even resemble the classics, and it was killing me. I wanted to prepare a lesson plan for her teacher on what books to teach. But I kept quiet. (This was back in my phase when I didn't want to look like I was from New York.) Then one day, Paris came home with a philosophy book that disputed the teachings of Jesus and suggested that Jesus may not have even existed, and that if He did, he was a cult leader. Paris decided to write a paper to refute that particular thesis. At that point, I decided to get involved.

We spent hours together. We talked about the synoptic Gospels. We talked about Josephus, the Hebrew historian. We talked about all kinds of things I didn't even know I knew. Two days later, Paris came home with her paper, *our* paper, in hand. We got a D! I got *acida* (Italian for "upset stomach") and Paris learned a very important lesson about what it means to meet with resistance.

KEEPERS OF THE GATE

Finally, brothers, whatever is true, whatever is noble, whatever is right, whatever is pure, whatever is lovely, whatever is admirable—if anything is excellent or praiseworthy—think about such things. (Phil. 4:8)

If you live alone, you are your own gatekeeper for what goes into your mind and heart. If you have a family, you are the gatekeeper for the household. I am watching what goes on in my house. I'm a domestic engineer. I'm trying to do a good job of it, but it's not easy. My kids are sharp, cultured, and they want to do and see things in the world. But I am teaching them to go against the flow. It's so good to have another gatekeeper at home, and I thank God for my husband. Frank is a perfect complement to me. If I were raising the kids alone, they'd have some serious issues. And if they were raised by Frank, they'd have even *more* issues. We're in this parenting thing together and we pray the children will turn out just fine—in spite of our shortcomings. Oh, how we need Jesus!

We're a team. Frank covers the math and I cover the English. He has a file system and I have a pile system. I'm loosey goosey and his approach is full of rules and regulations and goal setting. I like going with the flow. Frank has banned consumption of soda, dessert, and television from all weekdays. I say, "Eat, drink, and be merry for tomorrow we may die." He thinks "early to bed and early to rise" is somewhere in the Bible. It's *not*.

We love it when Frank goes out of town. When he is away, you can find the kids and me strolling through Target or getting ice cream on a Wednesday night after church. When Frank is out of town, the kids ask, "Mommy, can we have chocolate cake?"

"Yes, children. Of course!"

"How much, Mommy?"

"All you can eat! Until you're sick!"

"We love you, Mommy!

"I know. And I love *you*!"

I thank the Lord for the good times and the laughter—yes, Frank laughs both with me and at me. I realize there are many homes that have not known family unity and joy in quite a long time. I meet women whose husbands deal with serious issues regarding pornography, alcohol, and other addictions. I'm not suggesting that we have control over everything in our houses, but we do have control over *many* things. Yes, we will meet resistance from within our own family when we hold the line regarding certain standards for our home. But the people to whom you gave birth should *not* be ordering you around. And they certainly shouldn't be setting the tone of your home. That is not the kind of resistance-training that will make you stronger. It will create havoc in your home if you allow it to continue. If you need to find a counselor or a pastor to talk through some issues so you can resume your God-given responsibility in the home, I pray you'll do so. Whatever you need to do to take back those reins and stand your post as the gatekeeper, do it without delay. The Lord will guide you.

CHRISTIANS IN THE MIX

If I am attainable, touchable, and reachable then I am right where Jesus was when He walked the earth. If I am human and remain teachable, then I am right where Jesus wants me to be. He walks with us in the messiness of life and the complexities of human relationships. We have the peace and security of His company as we take the leap of faith and decide to go public with our beliefs. I love that God is raising up Christians in unexpected places. I am so appreciative of strong, vibrant believers who do not shy away from "the mix" of the world. I'm so grateful for the Christian Bikers Association. I admire Cops for Christ. I love the ministry Campus Crusade has to fashion models. I was comforted to know Commander Husband of the space shuttle *Columbia* was a devout believer. I am thrilled to read about the actors on Broadway or in Hollywood who are living out their faith. Even though their art and gifts speak for themselves, their passion for Jesus speaks loudest.

It is equally powerful to see the women in my weekly neighborhood Bible study "go public" with their faith. I didn't have to scold them and say, "Stop this ungodly behavior or cut out that wrong attitude." (And *they* continue to overlook *my* shortcomings.) The Holy Spirit does a much better job than we do when it comes to instructing others. Some of the women from the local study have said to me, "You know, Ellie, I'm not so comfortable anymore with that group of friends or with that brand of humor. I'm no longer allowing garbage TV and we are turning it off when we eat. And I'm certainly paying more attention to what comes in the house with my kids."

"At one time we too were foolish,.disobedient, deceived and enslaved by all kinds of passions and pleasures" (Titus 3:3).

Notice Paul uses the wording "at one time." When we take the leap of faith, we are going against the flow of all we once knew as familiar, comfortable, and self-gratifying. For the Christian, "at one time" is past; it is history. Nonbelievers continue to live like that in the present tense. I can love them, I can pray for them, but I'm not there anymore. The women in my Bible study are encountering opposition as they go against the flow, but it is making them stronger and wiser, and they are experiencing deep joy they have never known before—even in the midst of life's troubles.

What troubles, you ask? *Deep* troubles! I'm not talking about burning dinner, running stockings, or missing the deadline for preschool registration. The wonderful women in our weekly gathering face many serious trials. Some are for a season and some have no end in sight. Either way, they all cause discouragement and sadness. We are learning to lay these burdens down and to stop playing Superwoman. The death of a child, an unfaithful husband, a suicidal teen, a miscarriage, a special needs child, a struggling second marriage, a parent with Alzheimer's, fertility procedures, the demise of a business, single parenting, harmful addictions, unwanted pregnancy, financial ruin.

And that's not to mention the issues of self-worth, or lack of it, we *all* struggle with. "Come to me, all you who are weary and burdened, and I will give you rest" (Matt. 11:28).

THE COST OF THE CROSS

Christian jewelry is a major industry nowadays. Cross key chains. Cross earrings. Cross necklaces. Cross insignia rings. What would it be like if the cross we hung around our neck was six feet tall? What if instead of tucking it under our shirt collar, we had to bring it along on a date, tote it to the PTA meeting or lay it beside us on the negotiating table at work?

What if you had to bring that cross with you when you met somebody for lunch who just went through the loss of a loved one? Would it guide the conversation? What if you brought the cross with you as you bid farewell to someone dying in the hospital? How would a large cross in your cart affect your temperament as you waited in a long line at the supermarket and you were running late for an appointment?

Crosses are often worn by people who have no concept of the sacredness of the crucifixion. The body of Jesus was broken for us—and in the same way, we must allow Him to break our hearts in order to see His life flourish in us. The Lord understands our honeymoon time of falling in love with Him. However, in our newborn exuberance, we sometimes overlook the fact that with this new invitation to live—there is also the invitation to die. We must die to ourselves to have true life. Everlasting life. "I have been crucified with Christ and I no longer live, but Christ lives in me. The life I live in the body, I live by faith in the Son of God, who loved me and gave himself for me" (Gal. 2:20).

In 2001, extremists known as the Taliban kidnapped a group of Christian missionaries in Afghanistan. Among those held hostage were two American women, Heather Mercer and Dayna Curry, whose dramatic rescue after three months in captivity led to a whirlwind book and speaking tour. Later that year, I had the privilege of hearing them share their amazing story at the nearly packed MCI Center in D.C. They shared what one would usually expect to hear in a Christian setting. God sent them to Afghanistan. God gave them a deep love for the people. God provided for them and protected them in their captivity. God returned them home safely. Their accounts were riveting and their desire to return is a miracle in itself. The Lord's ways are wondrous.

What I did *not* expect to hear was something very personal that Heather shared regarding her ordeal. Toward the end of her talk, she listed some of the conditions, the fears, the indignities, and the mental aerobics she and her friends experienced at the hands of the Taliban. She then related that worse than *all* of those things, more painful to her heart than *anything* else, was the friction and discord she had with Dayna. How painfully honest and transparent. How disarming. And how universally true. We all have memories of difficult seasons and harsh words with those we cherish and spend a great deal of time with. I don't know if these young women experienced tension over whether or not to escape, whether or not to share food rations or whether or not to sign a forced confession. The details are not of import. What struck me was the powerful reminder that we are all sinners, all prone to self-preservation, all infected by the deadly sin called pride. Heather and Dayna have referred to themselves as "Prisoners of Hope." Jesus is our *only* hope to escape from our own similar prisons of selfishness and pride.

Is there no one who can do anything for me? Isn't that the real question?

The answer, thank God, is that Jesus Christ can and does. He acted to set things right in this life of contradictions where I want to serve God with all my heart and mind, but am pulled by the influence of sin to do something totally different. (Rom. 7:24–25 MSG)

I've considered writing a book titled, *You Can't Kill Me, I'm Already Dead.* That's actually the spiritual plateau I need to reach in order to fully understand my calling and freely offer my gifts to others. The world is not encouraging me to put others first, to be a servant, or to die to my own will. Instead, I am told, "Live it up. You only live once. Have it your way. Do what's good for you. Be your own boss." Like it or not, the road to knowing Jesus more intimately is a one-way road to the cross. It's a narrow road. And a lonely one at times.

Jesus said, "If anyone would come after me, he must deny himself and take up his cross and follow me" (Matt. 16:24). When we take up the cross, we might have our motives and actions misjudged. When we take up the cross, we might endure public mocking and ridicule. By the same token, when we take up the cross, we might also find ourselves loving people who are "not lovable" and forgiving people who "don't deserve" to be forgiven. That's what Jesus did.

A pastor once challenged his congregation not to defend themselves for an entire week. The following Sunday, he asked anybody who completed the task to stand. No one stood. I would be one of those who remained seated. Don't defend, explain, or justify myself for an entire week? Who wants to do *that*? We want to defend ourselves. We feel compelled to take the stand. We want to call the entire prayer chain with our version of the story.

When we moved to northern Virginia, I threw myself fully and wholeheartedly into serving at a Christian school. I quickly became the PTF president and a founding member of the school board. Four years and hundreds of volunteer hours later, I left the PTF, the school board, and along with half of the attending families, we withdrew our children from the school. The fourth and final spring on the campus was filled with backroom politics I had never before witnessed in a Christian setting. Relationships and reputations quickly deteriorated. It was painful and the Lord was grieved. I was maligned, my motives were questioned, and my "assertive" style was certainly not appreciated by some. I was hurt, disillusioned, embarrassed, and angry. Regretfully, I contributed to the hurt. I wanted to have my day in court and I wanted to be vindicated. I wanted to shake my fist. After all, I had enough "inside information" to set the record straight. Frank counseled me to leave quietly without a further word of defense, explanation, or retribution. I clung tightly to Exodus 14:14: "The LORD will fight for you while you keep silent" (NASB). I allowed the Lord to nurse my deep wounds that summer and I remained silent. That fall, God gave me back my speaking ministry—this time, on a national scale.

When I was young and immature (I'm no longer *young*), I thought the abundant life meant the great life—one free of any heartache and full of "success." Now I know it is an abundance of the heart. An ability to enjoy the richness of Christ and all that He is. As I grow closer to God, I cry harder. I feel deeper. I look higher. I am more sorrowful about what's going on in Timbuktu. I pay more attention to the channel that shows a little child in a war-torn refugee camp. I look at my relatives with an eye for their soul and not just an ear for their words. I listen longer and talk less (yes, I know ... *hard* to believe). I see the fruit of letting my children know the reality of Jesus and the power in His people. I am keenly aware of His heart for the strangers who cross my path. Our hearts need to break over the things that break God's heart. Your heart will certainly be moved if you allow the Holy Spirit access to *all* of your mind, heart, and soul. Your new heart will become fully evident to you and those around you. And you will thank God for the tender changes.

I laugh out loud when I hear people say Christianity is a crutch for the weak. Oh, *really?* A crutch? I don't think so. Turn the other cheek, give the shirt off your back, walk the extra mile, think of others as better than yourself? I rather liked it when Ellie did things Ellie's way. Said things that I wanted, to whom I wanted, when I wanted. Christianity cramps my style! It's easier and more natural to take charge—call the shots—be your own boss (and the boss of others). Luci Swindoll says, "The thing that controlling Christians and God have in common is that they both love you and have a plan for your life." We must be willing to yield—to "decrease" so that the Holy Spirit might "increase." However, yielding is hard work. It's not in my nature. It's certainly not part of my culture. I'm told to get out front and not to look back.

When you take up the cross, you will obey commands that you would never choose for yourself. When you take up the cross, you will no longer use power to promote yourself. When you take up the cross, you will see loved ones reject God in front of your very eyes. You'll have your words distorted, and you'll have your words used against you. You'll experience trusted friends turning into enemies. You will experience grief that no one can ever understand. When you take up the cross, you may even feel forsaken by God at times. If you feel any or all of these things, then you're in good company. This was the testimony of the men and women of the early church whose tears and trials blazed a trail for our faith to follow.

> We want each of you to show this same diligence to the very end, in order to make your hope sure. We do not want you to become lazy, but to imitate those who through faith and patience inherit what has been promised.
> (Heb. 6:11–12)

CHAPTER NINE

THIRTY-ONE MILES

Eunice had been diagnosed with a terminal illness and was told she had three months to live. She was seventy-six, had never married, and her only family was church family. As she was getting her things in order, she contacted her pastor and requested that he meet with her to discuss her final wishes. She told him what songs she wanted sung at the service, which scriptures she would like read, and what dress she wanted to be buried in with her favorite Bible resting in her arms. When everything was in order and the pastor was preparing to leave, Eunice announced, "There's one more thing, Pastor," she said intently.

"What's that?" he inquired.

"This is very important," the woman continued. "I want to be buried with a fork in my right hand." The pastor quizzically looked at her, not knowing quite what to say.

"That surprises you, doesn't it?" she asked with a smile.

"Well, to be honest Eunice, I *am* pretty curious about your request," said the pastor.

She took a deep breath and explained further, "When I

was a little girl growing up in the south, Sunday was church meetin' day. We traveled a while to get there and once we got there—we stayed put all day long. After Sunday school and the service, we always stayed at church for those amazing potluck dinners. The women served and the men cleaned up, and when they said 'Keep your fork,' that meant something better was coming. Not pudding or Jell-O, but velvety chocolate cake or deep-dish apple pie. Pastor, it may seem silly, but I want people at my funeral to see the fork in my hand, and I want you to remind them 'something better's coming.' You tell them Eunice said, 'The best is yet to come.'"

The pastor's eyes welled up with tears of joy as he hugged Eunice goodbye. He knew she had grasped the idea of heaven like very few had. Two months later at the funeral, those who walked by Eunice's casket saw the pretty dress she was wearing and her favorite Bible neatly placed in her arms. And then they saw the fork in her right hand. The pastor just smiled quietly and observed their puzzled looks as they returned to their seats. He heard more than one congregant whisper, "What's with the fork?"

During his message, the pastor told the people of the conversation he had with Eunice shortly before she died. He explained the fork and what it symbolized to her. And then he concluded, "I doubt any of us will ever forget the picture of faith we've seen here today. In fact, the next time you're told to "keep your fork" I hope you'll think of Eunice. For the believer, death is not final. It is God's way of saying, 'The table is ready, and the best is yet to come!'"

ANTICIPATING GOD'S FAITHFULNESS

I am challenged by that story because it reminds me that God is preparing us to move forward into greater things tomorrow than we experienced today. We must anticipate His work in our lives and expect Him to get us through our current trials, thoroughly convinced the best is yet to come. Why? Scripture says, "He who doubts is like a wave of the sea, blown and tossed by the wind. That man should not think he will receive anything from the Lord; he is a double-minded man, unstable in all he does" (James 1:6–8). Have you ever tossed and turned throughout the night worrying about the same problem you prayed about before going to bed? Have you ever crossed your fingers, hoping God will "show up" in your situation? Or are you confidently anticipating that He is at work, despite the evidence to the contrary? We must wait for His plans to fall into place according to His timing.

Unfortunately, we often lack a sense of excitement and confidence in what God is up to. I get the last hole punched on my salon card and I'm excited about a free haircut. I get an unexpected upgrade at the rental car or hotel counter and I'm thrilled. How much more so should Christians be excited about what our heavenly Father has in store for us!

You've probably experienced what it's like to count the days waiting for something special to happen like a vacation, a reunion, or a wedding. Maybe you've known the thrill of waiting for the arrival of a new baby. I like the true story about the woman who began having her baby in the car on the way to the hospital. In desperation, this woman's husband frantically wheeled onto the curb at the emergency room front door and yelled for help. As the emergency room staff created a makeshift delivery room in the backseat, the nurse tried comforting the sobbing mother who was obviously embarrassed by the ordeal. This was not how she had anticipated this long-awaited moment. "Don't worry, honey," the nurse said, patting her hand. "This kind of thing happens all the time. Just last year a woman had her baby on the front lawn of the hospital." The flustered mother didn't appear comforted at all. She just sobbed harder and said, "That was *me!*"

When the Israelites gathered their belongings on the morning they would cross the Jordan River, they were exhilarated. They had no idea how the details would come together, but they knew something big was about to happen. They would meet God there. God would meet *them.* The day had finally arrived.

> "Now then, choose twelve men from the tribes of Israel, one from each tribe. And as soon as the priests who carry the ark of the Lord—the Lord of all the earth—set foot in the Jordan, its waters flowing downstream will be cut off and stand up in a heap." So when the people broke camp to cross the Jordan, the priests carrying the ark of the covenant went ahead of them. (Josh. 3:12–14)

When we approach our current situation with the expectation that we will meet God there, everything changes. All things become possible when God shows up. As the Lord told the prophet Habakkuk, "Look at the nations and watch—and be utterly amazed. For I am going to do something in your days that you would not believe, even if you were told" (1:5).

PRAYER OF FAITH

One way we need to affirm our sense of expectation is in the way we approach God in prayer. Sometimes our prayers are so general that we would be hard pressed to tell if God answered them or not. We ask God for broad stroked blessings on a specific individual, but some are reluctant to be more specific in their requests. If that individual doesn't meet with calamity in the coming week we might assume that he or she was blessed in some fashion in response to our prayer. Yes, we ultimately desire God's will in every situation and pray toward that end, but does our lack of specificity belie a hesitant faith? The Israelites assembled together that morning to get a specific answer to a specific request. They needed to get across the river. God wanted them to get across the river. More importantly, He would help them to do it by faith.

Many of us apprehensively walk to the riverbank of our own issue, knowing we must somehow get across to the other side of our problem. When we ask for a general sense of blessing instead of getting to the root of our problem we leave the *real* work of getting across that river on our own to-do list instead of asking and believing that God will take us across. Don't misunderstand; I want God to bless me. I seek His blessing and favor on my life. But there are times when I have a specific need, and I must zero in on that request in full assurance of faith, believing that He hears me and He is already at work doing something about my concern. How or when He chooses to do it is out of my control. I sometimes question His methods and His timing but I have complete confidence in His goodness and mercy. What matters is that I believe He *will* help me cross any and every river, obstacle, and hurdle.

THE "AS SOON AS" PRINCIPLE

Joshua was only a young adult when he left Egypt along with two million other Hebrews. However, he must have made quite an impression serving as Moses' personal assistant. He was a man of faith and extraordinary courage, which made him the obvious choice for Moses' successor when Moses died. Even though he was around seventy-five years old at the time that he assumed his leadership role, he was still considered by some to be a youngster.

When he stood before the ranks of Israelites, Joshua detailed exactly what would happen before the crossing took place. The waters would keep flowing until the priests entered the river. God required more than just the dipping of toes in the water. They had to go all the way in. The Bible says "as soon as" the priests' feet touched the water's edge, the unbelievable happened. Get ready to be amazed!

Now the Jordan is at flood stage all during harvest. Yet as soon as the priests who carried the ark reached the Jordan and their feet touched the water's edge, the water from upstream stopped flowing. It piled up in a heap a great distance away, at a town called Adam. (Josh. 3:15–16)

Did you notice that the Bible says the headwaters "piled up in a heap a great distance away"? Although it happened "as soon as" the priests entered the water, just as God promised, it didn't happen right where they were. The town of Adam was thirty-one miles away from the spot where Israel crossed the Jordan. That meant the headwaters would have to flow for thirty-one miles after God supernaturally dammed the river at Adam. For thirty-one miles, the people of Israel had to hold onto hope.

Imagine the priests shouldering the ark, six on one side, six on the other, with Joshua at the helm shouting orders over the rush of water. The river current was strong, overflowing with bitterly cold current. The priests touched their feet in the water and submerged their legs in the icy torrent as the water rushed around them. There was no immediate change in the water level. The priests must have been murmuring, "Can you spell C-O-L-D, Joshua? Hello! Where is Moses now?"

I imagine the dialogue going on inside of Joshua's head to be something like, "God, this would be a *really* good time for you to come through. It's my first full day on the job, being the new kid on the block and all, and you know Lord—these people don't really respect me just yet ... ."

But God had promised him, "Today I will begin to exalt you in the eyes of all Israel, so they may know that I am with you as I was with Moses" (3:7). (There God goes again exalting a mere human and adding greatness to his reputation.) Did Joshua wonder if he'd heard God wrong as everyone stood in the bone-chilling rush? Did he misunderstand God's instruction? No e-mail alert. No cell phone service. No fax. No CB or walkie-talkie to reassure him, "Ten-four, Big Josh, the water's stopped in a big ol' heap up here in Adam. Don't worry, good buddy. It'll all be over soon."

Though Joshua and the priests had no way of knowing what God had done or how long they would have to stand, they trusted by faith and they stood. They stood as thirty-one miles of rushing water went by. Remember, the Jordan River was at flood stage; the water was not shallow.

What are *your* thirty-one miles? What trouble is swirling around your ankles or up to your ears and paralyzing *your* faith? What is making you fear that you might drown? Do you have the faith to wait thirty-one miles to see the incredible work of God unfold in *His* time? Do you believe that God began to work on your behalf "as soon as" you asked for help even though you cannot see help on the horizon?

When we look around at our torrent of trouble we are tempted to think, "God hasn't answered me." Yes, He has. In His time. In His way. Did God fulfill what He promised Joshua? Yes, God began working as soon as the priests' feet touched the water; Joshua just didn't know it yet. The evidence of God's power and presence is not always visible, but we can be sure He is at work. Remember, we are overcomers. We are overcoming every obstacle in life. The Bible says, "In all these things we are more than conquerors through him who loved us" (Rom. 8:37). Do you have the faith to stand through thirty-one miles of a wayward child, a daunting health report, financial loss, a tough marriage? Can you stand? Will you stand?

The foundation of the Twin Towers was the only structure to survive the total devastation of 9/11. In fact, engineers determined the original foundations were structurally sound enough to be used again. Those strong foundations refused to be moved, but they also protected the entire area of lower Manhattan. Few people realize that the towers were built on an area that was once beneath the Hudson River. According to a *New York Times* article in the summer of 2003, the walls connected to the foundation kept the force of the Hudson River from swallowing Lower Manhattan.

With a foundation like Jesus, we too can stand the incredible pressures of life's greatest tragedies and face our future with confidence. And we can bring a sense of stability, safety, and peace to those whose lives touch ours. The Bible says our feet are firmly planted in God's grace and nothing can shake us.

My hope is built on nothing less
Than Jesus' blood and righteousness.
I dare not trust the sweetest frame,
But wholly lean on Jesus' name.

On Christ the solid rock I stand
All other ground is sinking sand.[8]

Darlene is a sophisticated, striking woman of means. She has a gorgeous house, a big boat, a handsome husband, beautiful children, a maid, a vacation home on Florida's coast and, better than all of that, Darlene invited Jesus into her heart five years ago. Upon closer inspection, one would discover some troubling things about Darlene's "perfect" life. Her house is in foreclosure, her boat was just auctioned off, her husband is a functional alcoholic and a gambler, her son was arrested for selling drugs and her sixteen-year-old daughter just became pregnant. I've witnessed a few people go from rags to riches but the ride down the *other* side of that mountain must be excruciating. My heart hurts for her, and the Lord often brings her to mind. She sends prayer requests from North Carolina and when she signs off on her emails, she *always* uses the words, "I stand." I do not believe God will allow Darlene to drown in her river of impossibilities. I believe God makes a way when we think all is lost. Will you stand? (Italics added below.)

"We have peace with God through our Lord Jesus Christ, through whom we have gained access by faith into this grace in which we now *stand*."
—Romans 5:1–2

"You *stand* by faith." —Romans 11:20

150

"He will *stand*, for the Lord is able to make him *stand*."

—Romans 14:4

"No temptation has seized you except what is common to man. And God is faithful; he will not let you be tempted beyond what you can bear. But when you are tempted, he will also provide a way out so that you can *stand* up under it."

—1 Corinthians 10:13

"Therefore, my dear brothers, *stand* firm. Let nothing move you. Always give yourselves fully to the work of the Lord, because you know that your labor in the Lord is not in vain."

—1 Corinthians 15:58

"Be on your guard; *stand* firm in the faith; be men of courage; be strong."

—1 Corinthians 16:13

"Now it is God who makes both us and you *stand* firm in Christ ... because it is by faith you *stand* firm."

—2 Corinthians 1:21, 24

"Put on the full armor of God so that you can take your *stand* against the devil's schemes. ... Therefore put on the full armor of God, so that when the day of evil comes, you may be able to *stand* your ground, and after you have done everything, to *stand*. *Stand* firm then, with the belt of truth buckled around your waist, with the breastplate of righteousness in place."

—Ephesians 6:11, 13–14

"Epaphras, who is one of you and a servant of Christ Jesus, sends greetings. He is always wrestling in prayer for you, that you may *stand* firm in all the will of God, mature and fully assured."

—Colossians 4:12

"So then, brothers, *stand* firm and hold to the teachings we passed on to you, whether by word of mouth or by letter."

—2 Thessalonians 2:15

CARRY ON

Maybe you *have* stood in a difficult place for a long time. Maybe you've grown a bit numb. Maybe you've started to doubt. Maybe you're wondering if God has forgotten you—or worse—that He sees your pain and refuses to respond. I have not personally known gut-wrenching tragedy. I have not been well acquainted with grief. I cannot say I have felt your pain, but Jesus certainly has. In that, we find comfort. I am so thankful we worship a God who wrapped Himself in flesh and blood in order to provide us with His Spirit.

A young Christian lady named Brenda was doing some rock-climbing in the mountains with her friends one Saturday morning. Halfway up the mountain, her left contact lens popped out. Unfortunately, she is close to being legally blind without contacts. To her relief, Brenda's best friend offered to stay with her while the rest of the group finished the climb. "We'll have lunch here and wait for you!" she yelled to the group. "We'll meet you guys on your way down and then we'll figure out what to do."

The girls carefully made their way to a nearby plateau and unpacked their lunches. Brenda was so disappointed. It was one of the first clear, spring days after a tough winter, and she had looked forward to this outing so much. But now, the anticipation of a perfect day was dashed. She prayed more out of habit than anything else, "Lord, the Bible says your eyes look to and fro throughout the whole earth, so do you think you could help me find my contact lens?" She giggled a moment and felt embarrassed about the request. About two hours later, her friends returned and they all continued down the second half of the mountain together.

As they reached the bottom, they crossed another hiking party on their way up the mountain. A handsome guy in shorts and hiking boots casually asked, "Anybody lose a contact lens?"

Brenda and her friends were astounded.

"I did!" Brenda cried. She couldn't believe it when he handed her the unscratched contact lens.

"How did you ever find a contact lens on this mountain?" she asked.

"Oh, it was easy. It was moving."

"Moving?" she asked bewildered.

He laughed and said, "You're not going to believe this, but an ant was carrying it. The reflection of the sun caught it just right and made it sparkle like a diamond from a distance." Everyone grinned widely, especially Brenda.

Brenda's father, a syndicated comic strip artist in Minneapolis heard the whole story and decided to capture her experience in his column. In that Sunday's newspaper, his comic strip depicted an ant shouldering a contact lens.

In the first frame, the weary ant looks frustrated and burdened. There was a little bubble above its head that conveyed the ant's sentiments.

"God, I don't know why you want me to carry this thing."

In the subsequent frames, the ant continues his objections. "It's very heavy. I can't eat it. And it's making me *really* hot."

And the final frame says, "But, God, … if you want me to carry it … I will."

Let me ask you—what is it that you have you been carrying? What has stolen some of your hope? What is pressuring you and squeezing the joy out of your life? What is pressing you up against the wall? For some, it's a marriage that seems to be running out of love. For others, it's singleness and that occasional sense of not belonging. It's an unreasonable boss. It's caring for an aging parent. It's a dead-end job. A mean-spirited in-law. A disabled child. An ugly habit. A disturbing memory.

Whatever it may be, you feel like saying to God, "I don't even know why I have to carry this. I don't see the good that can come out of it and I feel tired and burdened. But, Lord … if you want me to … , I'll carry it."

When the world sees you standing in the chilly waters for thirty-one miles, carrying your burden, you'll be chastised for being a fool. *You don't have to do this, you know? It's time for you to think about yourself. It's time for you to worry about number one. You have taken as much as you can bear. Don't put yourself out. That's enough. Walk away. Give up. Stop being used. It's time for you to sit down and take a break.* And yet, Jesus says to stand. The waters *will* pass. He *will* help us to carry what we are sure we can no longer bear. "You turned my wailing into dancing; you removed my sackcloth and clothed me with joy" (Ps. 30:11).

Yet I Will Rejoice

The leap of faith is a choice. We make a choice to stand. Not everyone around us is choosing to take that leap. Some are scampering out of the torrent so quickly they never get to develop or flex their spiritual muscles. They don't know what they're capable of handling because they've never committed to staying in a situation that tries their faith. Most people run from the pruning shears, the refiner's fire, and the potter's firm grip. It's a sad commentary of American values when a bestseller entitled *Starter*

Marriages explains the trend to experience a spouse for a short season.

God understands our doubts, but He delights in our obedience. "If anyone chooses to do God's will, he will find out whether my teaching comes from God or whether I speak on my own," Jesus said in John 7:17. Obedience is appreciated when it is freely chosen, not when it is coerced. It's wonderful when my children obey because they choose to obey me, not under compulsion. Do we only love God when things are going our way—or can we, like Habakkuk, declare "Though the fig tree does not bud and there are no grapes on the vines, though the olive crop fails and the fields produce no food, though there are no sheep in the pen and no cattle in the stalls, yet I will rejoice in the LORD, I will be joyful in God my Savior" (Hab. 3:17–18).

THIS IS A TEST

"Consider it pure joy, my brothers, whenever you face trials of many kinds, because you know that the testing of your faith develops perseverance" (James 1:2–3). *Test* is another one of those words like *obedience* that doesn't sit well with me. I don't want any more tests. "Please, God, I am finished with school. I'm too old for tests"

"No, you're not," He lovingly responds.

The only survivor of a shipwreck was put to the ultimate test when he washed up on a desert island. He gathered a few materials remaining from the ship to build a little hut to shelter him from the elements. Days and then weeks went by with little food and no sign of help. One day when he returned from one of his scavenger hunts during a massive storm, he saw a huge lightning bolt strike his hut. He watched helplessly as it went up in flames. He sank to his knees and cried out, "God, what are you doing to me? The only protection I have is gone and now I'm going to die! Where are you? What are you thinking?"

An hour later, a ship came into view and some sailors rowed a small boat onto the shore to rescue him. The bewildered and exhausted man asked them, "How did you know I was here? No vessel has come this way in almost a month." They looked at him incredulously and replied, "Well, we saw your smoke signal asking for help."

Where are you, God?
"Right beside you."
How could you, God?
"I have a greater plan than you know."
When, God?
"At the perfect time."

Sometimes what we think is disaster is a blessing in disguise. Sometimes what we think is the end is just the beginning. What we think is bad news is really good news. Joseph gives us a glimpse of how God works all things together for our good when he declared to the brothers who sold him to slave traders, "You intended to harm me, but God intended it for good to accomplish what is now being done, the saving of many lives" (Gen. 50:20). Little did they know their baby brother would be taken to Egypt, rise to power in the house of Pharaoh, and save their lives during a national famine. They could not have conceived of it in their wildest imaginings. But God did.

When a child thinks it's the end of the world because she wasn't invited to a party, a wise parent can help because the parent has a much broader, clearer perspective than the child. In the same way, God reminds us that whatever we're going through is often not the catastrophe we think it is. It's easy to get discouraged when things are going badly, but don't lose heart, because God is always at work in our lives. Always. For every negative thing that we have to say, God has a positive response (paraphrased):

We say, *It's impossible.*
God says, "It's all possible with me." (Luke 1:37)

We say, *I'm too tired.*
God says, "I will give you rest." (Matt. 11:28)

We say, *Nobody loves me.*
God says, "I love you with an everlasting love." (Jer. 31:3)

We say, *But I can't go on.*
God says, "My grace is sufficient." (2 Cor. 12:9)

We say, *I can't figure things out.*
God says, "I'm going to direct all your steps." (Prov. 3:5–6)

We say, *I can't do it.*
God says, "You can do all things through Me." (Phil. 4:13)

We say, *I'm not able.*
God says, "I am able; I'm God." (2 Cor. 9:8)

We say, *I can't forgive myself.*
God says, "But I have forgiven you." (1 John 1:9)

We say, *I can't manage.*
God says, "I will supply every need." (Phil. 4:19)

We say, *I'm not smart enough.*
And He says, "I will give you the wisdom you need." (James 1:5)

We say, *I'm afraid.*
God says, "I've not given you a spirit of fear." (2 Tim. 1:7)

We say, *I don't have enough faith.*
God says, "I have given everyone a measure of faith." (Rom. 12:3)

PERFECT TIMING

God is never late. He might not act within the grid of your personal planner, but He's never late. "There has never been the slightest doubt in my mind that the God who started this great work in you would keep at it and bring it to a flourishing finish on the very day Christ Jesus appears" (Phil. 1:6 MSG). Spouses who won't come to church, work situations that never seem to get any better. When we consider our concerns, we must know that God will finish the work He began. At the same time, our greatest temptation is to want to help God "fix" it. We're fixers, aren't we? Give us a glue gun and some tape and we'll fix it. In many instances, God requests a "hands-off approach" so He can *truly* fix what is cracked or broken.

Go Ahead and Break My Heart

My abundantly gifted friend Kathy Troccoli has experienced a great deal of heartache. She has freely discussed her trials with many hundreds of thousands during almost twenty-five years of sharing her gifts throughout the U.S. and in Europe, Africa, and Israel. I've been so proud to witness her growth from pop singer to balladeer, from award show host to conference speaker, and from writing songs to writing books and Bible studies. To watch Kathy on a platform with her powerhouse vocals, her command of 20,000 women, her designer suit, and her Hollywood smile, one would never guess what harrowing rivers of impossibilities she has crossed. Depression, anger, ten years of bulimia, bankruptcy, the loss of both parents to the ravages of cancer, poor relationship choices, poor business choices, poor personal choices, long hours in counseling. But the very places Kathy was wounded are the same places where her audiences find comfort. God has used her scars to bring healing. He confounds our ways.

Our friendship began early in 1991, when her dear mother's cancer had spread. We walked through that season together and became close rather quickly. Watching the dying process causes one to give more time and attention to living. Kathy prayed for Josephine Troccoli's healing every single day—several times a day—twice in the same hour. She prayed in the studio, she prayed in the car, she prayed at church, she prayed when Frank and I took her out for dinner. The thing I will never forget about that year was that Kathy prayed for her mom's healing until that last breath. Then Kathy thanked the Lord because she realized the healing had finally come. Her lyrics to a poignant song, "Break My Heart," give valuable insight as to how she not only survived the storms—but chose to embrace them:

It's been the rain, it's been the storms.
It's been the days when I've been worn
That I have found you Lord,
That I have seen you Father.
It's in the pain that I have grown
Through all the sorrow I have known,
But if that's what it takes
for you to lead me this far ...
Go ahead and break my heart. [9]

PART FOUR

CHAPTER TEN

WHAT DO THESE STONES MEAN?

LILY PAD LIVING

What happens when we get to the other side of the river of impossibility? After we take a leap of faith most of us would expect a little rest, a little relaxation. Or at the least, a long nap. I'm afraid not. As the Israelites discovered after crossing the Jordan, we, too, soon realize there is more than one leap of faith in our future. Read a bit further beyond chapter three in Joshua and you'll discover that they didn't cruise on into the Promised Land after their successful river crossing. As it turns out, there were many more "rivers of impossibility" they would encounter before they "entered in." God didn't just hand over the keys to the Promised Land. Before they even had time to rest, Israel had to go against giants in Jericho. Conquering Canaan was one hard-fought battle after another in order to secure their boundaries.

Life has particular seasons where it seems as though all of our energy is spent clearing hurdles. Crossing the river is revitalizing, but another challenge awaits us just around the bend. Getting through a difficult childbirth, healing from a serious illness, or climbing your way out of debt is rewarding and well worth celebrating, but there will be other difficulties that come your way. Be assured. I like to think of the leap of faith as "lily pad living"—if we stay too long in our comfort zones we get lazy, things start to grow where they shouldn't, and the swamp starts to have curious odors. We must be ready and willing for the next leap.

At the end of each leap, no matter what challenge awaits us, we will have gained a greater knowledge of God's character than we ever had before. Our confidence in His promises will increase with the knowledge that He is utterly reliable and entirely trustworthy. Most importantly, we'll be able to pass along these same promises with full assurance to future generations.

A FAITHFUL GOD

When the whole nation had finished crossing the Jordan, the LORD said to Joshua, "Choose twelve men from among the people, one from each tribe, and tell them to take up twelve stones from the middle of the Jordan from right where the priests stood and to carry them over with you and put them down at the place where you stay tonight." So Joshua called together the twelve men he had appointed from the Israelites, one from each tribe. (Josh. 4:1–4)

He said to the Israelites, "In the future when your descendants ask their fathers, 'What do these stones mean?' tell them, 'Israel crossed the Jordan on dry ground.'" (Josh. 4:21–22)

Picture the men of Israel shouldering those huge stones. These are not the river rocks used to circle a campfire. They placed massive boulders in the middle of the camp for everyone to see. Can't you just hear the speculation coursing through the camp? *What are these guys doing? What are they building? Did you see the size of those stones?* Therefore, the Lord explained His unusual request. This was a sign—as much for those standing there that day as for future generations they would never know—that God's faithfulness is as indomitable and unmoving as the boulders before them. Israel captured the moment and commemorated God's faithfulness. Then they left it behind to inspire others and continued on their way.

It took considerable time and effort for Israel to leave something behind—the journey came to a halt. Sweat beaded on their foreheads and backs as they hauled large stones from the middle of the river. Israel didn't tersely scribble their story in the sandy riverbank to be washed away within a few days. They didn't scoop together pebbles of praise to memorialize the miracle of God. They shouldered boulder-sized gratitude in order to accurately convey the enormity of what God did that day so that when the question was asked, "What do these stones mean?" the answer would be swift and evident. These stones? They mean trust and triumph. They mean life. They mean deliverance. They mean there's a hope for the future.

You see, we all need reminders of God's powerful work in the past to give us faith for the future. Notice what Joshua said to the Israelites, "Tell them, 'Israel crossed the Jordan on dry ground.' For the Lord your God dried up the Jordan before you until you had crossed over. The Lord your God did to the Jordan just what he had done to the Red Sea when he dried it up before us until we had crossed over" (Josh. 4:23). Joshua reminded the people that God didn't miraculously save them from the Red Sea only to let them drown in the Jordan River. He was faithful in the past—why would He change His plans now? Their God would continue to look after them in the future, just as He had in the past.

Why is He faithful? "He did this so that all the peoples of the earth might know that the hand of the LORD is powerful and so that you might always fear the LORD your God" (Josh. 4:24). We, too, should look for ways to creatively communicate the message of God's faithfulness to those around us. When others witness the evidence of God's mighty work on our behalf, it gives God tremendous glory. At the same time, it inspires the committed Christian—and even the most casual observer—to recognize the power of God in our midst. Scripture eloquently speaks of the mighty, powerful hand of God. Consider the powerful hand of conviction in Psalm 32:4. Marvel at the mighty hand of deliverance in Exodus 13:3 and the powerful hand that inspired David in 1 Chronicles 28:19. Because this *same* hand guides and guards our lives, my children can see that yesterday's Y2K scare was not the end of the world, and terrorism is not going to make us run away for fear of what may happen tomorrow.

So, where *is* the safest place in the world? In God's will. No matter where we are geographically, we have to remember that we are only and always safe inside of His will, cupped in His caring hands, where we rest knowing we are loved and protected.

One of the great things about moving near Washington D.C. is that I've become quite a patriot. I take friends to visit the memorials, and I can recite the history of the Washington Monument. For instance, I learned that a third of the way up the Monument the limestone changes color because the building process ceased abruptly during the Civil War, and they couldn't match the stone when the war concluded. I love picturing President Lincoln walking around the Monument as he often did at night, hands clasped behind his back, with his long shadowy frame pacing in the evening haze as he thought and prayed about a war that deeply scarred America.

On a professional (secular) tour, the articulate and highly knowledgeable guide explained that small pocket Bibles were once standard military issue. Most surprising, he informed us that the architects originally laid out the foundation of Washington in the shape of a cross. Perfectly symmetrical, perfectly equidistant. At the heart of the cross: the Washington Monument. At the head of the cross: the Capitol. At the foot of the cross: the Lincoln Memorial. At the right hand: the White House. At the left hand: the Jefferson Memorial. The headquarters of

America was designed and laid out in the configuration of the cross. Did they erase that from *your* history book? They erased it from mine.

If we're not careful, we can create some revisionist history of our own. We might be tempted to leave God out of the picture when we get together for family reunions or when we celebrate holidays. It's easy to do and the consequences are tragic. We tend to frame our family stories in such a way that our narratives spotlight off-color lore regarding who was a happy drunk, who was a charming womanizer and who was a likeable bigot. History, in essence, is "His story." As believers, we must set crooked paths straight and establish standards that may have not previously existed. We must never forget that the mighty hand of God is ultimately the only worthy focal point of our story.

Today, when we think of the Washington Monument and the National Mall and the Capitol we think about the people who work there. Ironically, these memorials were initially crafted to symbolize an even bigger picture. They were to teach us something *about* God and His centrality in our country. Likewise, the stone memorial was not *about* the Israelites or a tribute to anything they had done. Certainly, the memorial they built was for their benefit and that of future generations, but it was never about *them*. The memorial was built to point future generations to the God who is "the same yesterday and today and forever" (Heb. 13:8).

LEST WE FORGET

Considering I've never been the crafty-type (bless those of you who own glue guns), I'm glad we no longer have to commemorate our Christian faith by building anything. Even so, people still ask us *What do these stones mean?* kinds of questions all the time. I'm referring to our modern day memorials. Our church traditions. Our spiritual sacraments. And our stories.

For example, children whisper to their parents during a church service, "Mom, Dad, why are we having baptism?" Neighbors and friends who didn't grow up in church wonder during communion, "What do the little pieces of bread mean? Why the cup?" When my own children asked me about the traditions in the church, I told them, "We do this because we need to remember." We do this so we won't forget. Jesus instructed the disciples on the night He was betrayed to celebrate the Lord's Supper. Why the cup? Why the broken bread? "Do this in remembrance of me" (Luke 22:19).

Remember. Remember. Remember. Some of us have lost the awe of traditions and sacraments. Some churches have minimized the importance of what it means to share communion with brothers and sisters in the faith. Some Christians have downplayed the powerful picture of baptism as just another event instead of recognizing the Gospel being portrayed before their eyes—buried with Christ and raised to walk in a brand new life. The world needs to see the spiritual meaning and hear the wonderful story behind the traditions and sacraments we may too often take for granted.

In ninth grade, I went to slumber parties with my Jewish girl-friends in Long Island, but I was also going with them to Sabbath and Seders. The story of God's faithfulness was retold through the reading of the *Haggadah* every year at Passover. With its special foods, songs, and customs, the Seder meal is the focal point of the Passover celebration. I remember sitting in a home, awestruck, listening to the opening words of the *Mah Ishtanah*—a series of questions posed by the youngest member at the meal.

"Why is this night different than any other night?"

"On all other nights ..." the answer began in chorus as they went on to recite, in Hebrew, the uniqueness of the meal. I didn't understand what they were saying, but one thing was clear. This night *was* different; from the youngest to the oldest, they had remembered.

In order for generation after generation to remember the foundations of our Christian faith, we have to tell the story. The good news of the Gospel is that we now remember that *one day* is different than any other day—the bright rays of the first Easter morning brought fulfillment to the Scriptures that God would send the Messiah to save us from sin. Why are the spiritual traditions of Christmas and Easter different from every other holiday? Why is there more to these celebrations than caroling and chocolate bunnies? Because even though the world may have forgotten, we remember.

THE POWER OF STORIES

A couple of my Jewish friends' grandparents had been in concentration camps during World War II. Their stories carved deep and lasting impressions on my young heart. It saddens me that the majority of today's young people have no idea where their grandparents were born, and many of them don't care about the value of family heritage. I love my grandmother's story. I cherish my grandfather's story. I learned them from my parents and grandparents, aunts and uncles. I tell these stories to my children to keep that rich tradition alive. Family is fascinating—and those bygone generations will never be replaced or rivaled. The loyalty, the work ethic, and the ways they used their hands to work, to prepare food, and to play are sadly foreign to most of us.

My paternal grandparents, Giuseppe and Elvira Mannarino, were born in southern Italy. They went to New York in 1907 to make a better life. My maternal grandparents, Rudolfo and Mercedes Bermani, were born in northern Italy. They went to New York in 1955 to be near their oldest daughter (my mother), Alessandra, who married an American (my father), Albert. Two years later, I came along and we lived in the same Brooklyn neighborhood where my Dad grew up. Boy, do I have stories! Okay, maybe just one for now ...

I was always curious about my father's deep repugnance of any and all references to the Mafia. My father never liked any form of media that glorified the Mafia. He always felt it degraded the two million Italians who arrived at Ellis Island between 1905 and 1915 to make honest livings through dedication, ingenuity, and backbreaking labor. He especially resented tongue-in-cheek humor from friends and neighbors insinuating he might be "one of the boys." Dad worked for Allstate Insurance for more than a decade, opened his own agency at the age of forty and worked hard to achieve success in suburbia. He went from a brownstone with chilly bathrooms to a grand colonial on a wooded acre, with a couple of houses in between. Dad wore crisp suits, sharp ties, and polished shoes. He had thick, wavy salt and pepper hair and he favored Old Spice. That he loved to drive large dark sedans, including a Lincoln Town car, only added to the stereotyping and the intrigue. *Was he or wasn't he?*

During a spring break, I visited Dad's older sister, Aunt Ida (with a memory like an elephant), and I dug for a deeper explanation behind his high sensitivity to the issue. Like thousands of other Italian men at that time, my grandfather made cane back chairs and sold blocks of ice. Grandma gave birth to eleven children and after the first few were born, a dream came true when my grandfather opened a small cigar business. When "The Black Hand" (an organization of corrupt Italian extortionists) told Grandpa they would provide his business with "protection" for a monthly charge, he refused them. After all, he had no reason to fear anyone. A week after he declined their "services" for the third time, they taught him a lesson. Cigars were planted in the shop without the proper import seal and band, which meant they were untaxed and illegal. A police inspector *happened* to come by and located the planted cigars. My grandfather was fined severely, and though he struggled to keep the business afloat, it was eventually destroyed by arson. My grandfather often repeated the unfortunate saga to his children. And now I have shared it with my own children who learned about injustice and personal convictions through the example of their great-grandfather who refused to yield to an evil regime.

Our family histories need to be told. Our children need to be reminded of the sacrifices that have been made so that they could enjoy certain comforts and privileges. Of course you may not receive much cooperation at first, but do you know what? The most amazing things begin to happen. Questions are asked, old photos come out of the closet, and a sense of pride and heritage is instilled.

I realize not everyone has family roots steeped in a rich spiritual history. As a first-generation Capital "C" Christian, let me remind you of the larger family of faith we share. From biblical heroes to more modern-day saints like Eric Liddel— the inspiration behind the movie, *Chariots of Fire*. He was a champion Olympic runner who gave up fame and fortune to serve as a missionary in China and died in a prison camp. Dietrich Bonhoeffer. Amy Carmichael. Jim Elliot. William Tyndale. John Wycliffe. Corrie ten Boom. These names, while they may not necessarily be familiar to you now, are part of the spiritual heritage of all Christians. Turn off the Fox sitcom and open the *Fox's Book of Martyrs*. Learn their stories. Let them inspire you to greater commitment as you realize deeper dimensions and multiple facets of God's faithfulness. Tell others about the long line of spiritual heroes from which you come and be proud to share the family name, Christian, alongside of them.

A LEGACY OF LOVE

Similarly, we should be concerned that our family and friends, as well as our larger spiritual family—the church, grow in their knowledge and understanding of God. The leaders of Israel built the memorial together because they crossed over together. They carried this sense of togetherness and unity with them into creating a memorial that would stand the test of time. They were thinking of future generations, not just themselves.

I pray the Lord says to me, "Well done, Ellie," when I meet Him in heaven. Not because I went to church, taught a Bible study, and tried to control my tongue, but because I pointed people to Him. The leap of faith is tied to our legacy because ultimately the leap is not about us. I love the opening sentence of Pastor Rick Warren's runaway bestseller, *The Purpose-Driven Life*: "It's not about you." What a relief! Our strong commitment to Christ should primarily be a blessing to other people. Taking the leap of faith and crossing over the river results in the desire to bring others with us to higher places in their relationship with God. We should have the sincere desire to help others and build them up in their faith. I'm taking that leap, and I am going to bring as many people as I can to the water's edge with me. I want God to be pleased to say to me, "Because of you, some people didn't get divorced. Because of you, some people were encouraged. Because of you, missionaries were born, marriages were strengthened, and the community was impacted."

In the same way, God's promise to Abraham was not just for him but also for a future multitude he would never meet. It was for an entire nation of people through whom the Messiah would eventually be born. God's abundant promises would supply Abraham, his family, and his servants and other people far beyond Abraham's death. The treasures, the power, the peace—all that we have in Christ—can affect so many beyond just ourselves and our families.

But if we don't genuinely care about people, we won't care much about building memorials or leaving legacies. We can't leave a meaningful legacy apart from a sincere heart of love. We can do good things for other people, but if we aren't motivated by love, we haven't progressed very far in our faith. We can head church committees, go to fundraisers, teach Sunday school, donate to Goodwill, buy cookies from Girl Scouts, and give blood on a regular basis. Yet the primary motivation behind everything we do needs to be love, or it's worth nothing. First Corinthians 13, the well-known "love chapter," makes it very clear. The leap of faith into all that God has for us profits us nothing if we miss love along the way. "If I have a faith that can move mountains, but have not love, I am nothing" (1 Cor. 13:2). Eugene Peterson translates the value of love into today's vernacular most eloquently:

> If I speak with human eloquence and angelic ecstasy but don't love, I'm nothing but the creaking of a rusty gate. If I speak God's Word with power, revealing all his mysteries and making everything plain as day, and if I have faith that says to a mountain, "Jump," and it jumps, but I don't love, I'm nothing.
>
> If I give everything I own to the poor and even go to the stake to be burned as a martyr, but I don't love, I've gotten nowhere. So, no

matter what I say, what I believe, and what I do, I'm bankrupt without love. (1 Cor. 13:1–3 MSG)

We must ask the Lord to grant us a heart filled with a deep love for others, especially within Christ's body, the church. The great English pastor and theologian, Charles Spurgeon, spoke with a friend who, despite his growing interest in the personal intellectual pursuit of God, insisted that he could pursue God aside from the encumbrances and complications of church attendance. As Spurgeon and his friend enjoyed the warmth from a fire in Spurgeon's study, the friend admitted, "I'm not so sure I'm comfortable sharing my private pursuit of God in a large group." While the fellow continued speaking, Spurgeon stepped closer to the fireplace and used a poker to take out one of the embers, knocking it to the floor. The men casually stared at the lone flickering ember a little while before it died.

At that moment, the young fellow off-handedly commented, "Well, that died pretty quickly out there on its own." Spurgeon, seizing the moment, was quick to make reference to why God created the church—so that no one's passion for God will die apart from the body.

We cannot afford to be Robinson Crusoe or Lone Ranger Christians. How can we hope to stand alone apart from the spiritual support we find within the body of believers, the church? To the contrary, Paul expresses his desire that we will all be "rooted and established in love" within the body of Christ (Eph. 3:17).

I have friends who claim, "God is everywhere. I can experience Him on the walking trail, on the golf course or in the kitchen." While those observations are true, it is exceedingly dangerous to fall into the growing ranks that maintain that they can seek God independently and exclusively on their own terms. We must participate and engage the other members of the body in order to experience a full range of motion in our faith. Our personal time with God, although it is essential to our growth as a Christian, cannot take the place of church life. It is understandable to feel conflicted about this topic if you have been deeply hurt by "the church." Although the church is composed of fallible humans, it is still beloved by God, and there are many genuine believers who are filled with integrity and love. C. S. Lewis referred to the church as God's "laboratory." It's where we learn the larger truths about life—giving us a wide array of experiences to help us grow and to challenge our selfish nature. Commitment to the church, both local and universal, is absolutely necessary for one to establish and maintain a healthy Christian life. The church is the bride of Christ. How foolish and rude we would be to ignore her.

His intent was that now, through the church, the manifold wisdom of God should be made known to the rulers and authorities in the heavenly realms, according to his eternal purpose which he accomplished in Christ Jesus our Lord. (Eph. 3:10–11)

CHAPTER ELEVEN

A LEGACY WORTH LEAVING

HERITAGE VERSUS LEGACY

At this point, you may say to yourself, "There's nothing significant about my story. In fact, if you knew my family history, it's hardly one I'd want to pass on to my children, my colleagues, or anyone else." I'd like to encourage you not to confuse your heritage with your legacy. Heritage is what you get, and legacy is what you give. Heritage is what's handed down to you. Legacy is what you leave. Every family's story has one thing in common—the good is mixed in with the bad. I am not responsible for my heritage. But the legacies we leave, the choices we make, are entirely up to us.

The Bible teaches that the "sins of the forefathers" will visit the third and fourth generations. I never knew what that meant until I had children. They're visiting, alright. In fact, they don't knock; they just come right in. I sometimes joke about my kids being perfect until they were eighteen—*ahem*—months. That's when they started displaying character traits from Frank's side of the family.

It isn't any better now that they're older. I dare say it's

getting worse. I look at things that really concern me about my children, and guess who I see? It's me! I didn't mean to pass on that bad habit or that poor attitude or that insecurity to my kids. I meant to leave that baggage behind. It seems my uncrucified flesh has quite a stench. I am a work in progress and my husband and kids wish I'd get on with it.

Yet, with all my warts, I thank God that my children will not share all of the same issues in their futures that I have struggled with in my past. With His help, I am overcoming many of those issues. I'm a better mother this year than last year, and I expect to show signs of improvement with every year of life.

We need to realize that there is an abundance of hope when it comes to our legacy. Without hope, we may as well give up trying to make a difference in anyone's lives. And some of us have done just that. *I'll never ... It will never ... It can never ... How could it? ...* Those unanswered questions in your mind are God's business. Remember from our study of Joshua that leaving a legacy is God's idea. Instead of renting a billboard or placing an ad to tell the world about His power and might, He wants people to "read" what He has done in your life and see God's power for themselves. Paul, when he left the church in Corinth to establish another church, left no doubt as to who would continue to convey the powerful message of the Gospel to the rest of those living in Corinth. He wrote to the church members, "You yourselves are our letter, written on our hearts, known and read by everybody. You show that you are a letter from Christ, the result of our ministry, written not with ink but with the Spirit of the living God, not on tablets of stone but on tablets of human hearts" (2 Cor. 3:2–3).

WHAT'S IN A NAME?

Before I moved to Virginia, I hosted a live radio talk show at a Christian station in New York. I loved interviewing both locally and nationally acclaimed guests. I was also receiving more invitations to speak. I was on the church women's leadership committee, and I had family nearby. Life was good. Life was busy. Life was comfortable.

When we moved, I had to give up my radio show. My local public speaking came to a halt. I found myself surrounded by women who looked like Barbie. I thought I could impress them with my "life experiences." No one cared. I thought I had some new ideas to offer. No one was interested. They thought I was too opinionated. These women were thin and accessorized. I wore lots of elastic. They dressed up to go to the bus stop. Me? I grabbed the cleanest pair of baggy sweats I could find. They were multi-tasking former executives. I was so pleased to learn how to send an attachment through the Internet.

After my precarious foray into the Christian school, I decided to exchange my chief hat for a mop at the local public school. Every week, I stuffed envelopes, sorted student assignments, and helped in the cafeteria. I opened milk cartons, mopped the floor and threw away lots of unrecognizable, chewed-on items. One night, as I was grocery shopping, this excited little second grader came running up to me pulling his mother with him. His mother was blonde, of course—wearing a designer suit and fresh from the office with her nine-hour pantyhose on. The child pointed and proudly introduced me, "Mommy, Mommy, it's the... *Cafeteria Lady*!" I cringed. I wanted to whip out my resume and tell her that I had taught high school English. That I held a Master's Degree in Literature. I wanted to tell her about my radio show. I wanted to say that I have organized and spoken at many retreats. That I knew CPR. That I played guitar and field hockey and the violin (okay—so maybe the violin lessons only lasted seven weeks). Standing there, thirty pounds overweight, wearing flats and an elastic waistband, I mustered up the biggest smile I could and said, "Yes, I'm the cafeteria lady. And how are you?" I was murmuring all the way home about how humiliated I felt when God suggested that I get over myself and learn to love the blonde women. The rest is an amazing testimony to His goodness when we are not good, and to His faithfulness when we are not faithful.

I learned a big lesson about my identity in Christ. I can be impressed with my reputation, job, or my contribution to society—with the secret hope that others will be impressed too. But I'm supposed to be dead. "For you *died*, and your life is now hidden with Christ in God" (Col. 3:3, emphasis added). My reputation rests solely on who I am in Christ. Ellie Lofaro is not as important as Ellie Christian.

What will others remember about you? Answer: not what you think. My kids are not going to remember Mom the radio show host, the author, or the speaker. I want my children to remember me as the woman who loved them unconditionally and invested all she had into their lives. "Ellie the Christian" is going to make a difference now and in future generations.

Are you ready for a quiz? Name the last four winners of the Nobel Peace Prize. How about the last three World Series winners? Name the last two Academy Award winners for best actor. How did you do? Now, try this one:

Think of three teachers who helped you in school. Name four people who taught you something worthwhile about life. Name four people who have made you feel appreciated. Name five people whose company you enjoy. What's the point? It's not our degrees. It's not our salaries. It's not our 1040 forms. Those things may earn us some kudos, but they don't make for a lasting legacy. It's not our rewards that count; it's relationships. All the time we spend in our offices trying to build our reputations and increase our net worth at the cost of neglecting our loved ones—will one day be revealed as foolishly wasted time. God is not so impressed with the awards because awards tarnish. Applause die down. Achievements are forgotten. Accolades and certificates turn to dust. The people who are significant in our lives are those who cared for us—the ones who showed concern. It's the person who told you that you were pretty when other people said you weren't. It's the person who said, "You can do it!" when others said, "You'll never make it." The one who took time to care is the one who lives on in your heart and mind. It's *that* person who has given you the gift of a legacy.

INVESTING IN OTHERS

I am indescribably blessed to be impacted by the legacy of a highly remarkable woman. I initially met Patsy Clairmont at a Women of Faith conference in 2000 and spent some quality time with her later that year. Patsy is one of the finest Christian communicators in the world. Her ability to combine the power of the Word with the power of laughter is, well … *powerful.* I have not seen many who combine the two as masterfully as Patsy does. Exactly six months from our first encounter and by God's divine appointment, we entered into a sacred covenant—a Paul and Timothy mentorship. We have visited several times and she has become a faithful correspondent.

> *Dear Ellie,*
>
> *I am about to enter the busiest season of my life, so know that at any point there is a lull on my end, that I will soon resurface. I am placing you during this time as one of my priorities.*
>
> *I want to focus on the area of balance, since your zeal may tend to run ahead of you. Contemplative moments give our busy moments content … otherwise we become little more than a rushing wind in an already stormy world.*
>
> *Your gifts are many, including a discerning spirit which I have noted in times we have been together. I believe God has great things planned for your future …*

Patsy had prayerfully decided to execute an eternal investment in another person. A younger woman in whom she saw potential—me. When I open my email inbox and see her name, I realize how Timothy must have felt whenever he received word from Paul—his mentor, father-figure, and friend.

> *Dear Ellie,*
>
> *I've been thinking that one of the equations the Lord has given to me to benefit you is my brokenness. While your life has not been charmed, it has been amazingly free of things many of us have been hampered by. The only way damage becomes of value is when the Lord redeems it. Then and only then, it takes on a divine characteristic of pure ministry. God has prepared you for ministry ... and now, for whatever ongoing reasons, He has given us each other.*

To understand how humbled I am by Patsy taking time to invest in, encourage, and direct my ministry—you need to know the magnitude of hers. She has addressed millions and is a best-selling author of numerous books. She's a devoted wife, mother, and grandma. That little body has a gigantic heart inside. I have learned so much from Patsy. Because she has made time in her whirlwind schedule to sow seeds into me, I am reminded of my responsibility to do the same for others. May her life-giving words of wisdom inspire you as well to create a deliberate strategy and allow the Holy Spirit to guide you as you invest in people God brings across your path.

Dear Ellie,

Thinking of you today and praying for your inner life—not your liver or your bladder—although we need those blessed too, but I'm praying for your focus and your peace. I pray for your integrity and your maturity.

I pray for enlightened eyes of the heart that you might see beyond words. I pray for heart-tenderness before you speak so that your conversations bring healing and not advice. And I pray for a growing awareness of Christ's presence in your daily-ness. May you rest your busy head on pillows full of sweet dreams and rise up to walk on straight paths.

May your heart grow in faithfulness and may you see His tender mercies on the right hand and the left hand. And may you lean into His Spirit all of your days. Amen.

I love you,
Patsy

THE DASH

Most tombstones are dated with two sets of numbers: the year of birth and year of death. In the middle of those two years is a short dash that represents life. Friendships. Love gained and lost. Laughter. Pain. Success. Failure. I am challenged by the idea of living our dash well. I want to live my dash with passion and purpose. Life has enough regrets. I want to minimize mine as I pursue God's ways and not my own. One particular fellow who lived his dash well was Butch O'Hare, from Chicago. A fighter pilot, Butch received a hero's medal in World War II for his bravery in a battle that changed history. Eleven of the twelve American planes from Butch's squadron had been shot down during fierce fighting. Butch's plane, with its bullet-ridden tail section, was the only one left to accomplish the mission. Despite sustaining heavy artillery fire and facing a nearly depleted fuel supply, Butch turned back toward the battlefield to drop a few more bombs. His determination to make one more run at the target with apparent disregard for his own safety turned the tide of this pivotal battle.

At that time, the government had designed special cameras strapped to the wings of the B-52 bombers to document flight patterns and learn more about the enemy's terrain. When the officials saw Butch's heroic, single-handed efforts on film, they decorated him with every conceivable honor. In 1949, a few years after the war ended, one of the busiest airports in America was named in his honor.

A couple of decades earlier, there was another fellow from Chicago who made his own claim to fame. His name was Easy Eddie—a lawyer for the notorious mobster Al Capone. It was Easy Eddie's job to keep Al Capone out of prison, and he did. A sharp attorney, Easy Eddie knew every loophole in the law, and Capone generously showed his appreciation for Easy Eddie's skills. His house, a gift from Capone, was the length of an entire city block and came complete with a butler, chauffeur, and a nanny for his young son.

Easy Eddie had everything anyone could want. Or so he thought. He loved his son dearly and had given him the best money could buy in terms of toys, clothes, and a good education. However, despite all he could afford for his son, he realized there was one thing he could never give him—a good name. Distraught over how corrupt he had allowed himself to become, he decided to change the legacy he would leave his son—to radically alter his "dash." But in order to give his son a name he could be proud of, Easy Eddie would have to go to the authorities and testify against Capone, the most dangerous man in the region. One month after his confession, Easy Eddie was shot dead on a dark Chicago street. However, he left his son with a greater hope for a good name. You see, Easy Eddie's last name was O'Hare, and the famed fighter pilot, Butch O'Hare, was Eddie's son. I don't know where Eddie O'Hare was in his journey of faith, but I'd like to think he made peace with his Creator. For all his failures, his ultimate success was leaving his son a good name and changing the course of his legacy.

A Parent's Greatest Gift

I'm from an ethnic culture that places children at the center of life. This propensity is not exclusive to any particular culture. For many, the children are *everything*. And often, when the baby comes, the sun rises and sets on that baby and everything and everyone becomes secondary. I realize it's a source of humor for some, but it's really quite unhealthy. There is the potential to create a very unbalanced scenario in any family where everything revolves around the children. My parents raised five children, looked at each other twenty-five years later, and wondered, "Who are you?" A year later, they were divorced. By God's grace, Frank and I will continue to navigate life together with Jesus at the helm and His living Word as our map. Our children will, God-willing, leave the house one day, and I will have committed a grave error if I have not made my relationship with Frank a priority.

One of the most important roles parents play in their children's lives is to equip them to make their own choices. I tell my kids all the time, "If you make godly choices, I'll smile with you. And if you make poor choices, I'll cry with you. But someday soon—the choices will be *yours.*" Our kids are on loan. We are stewards. I plan to equip my children as well as I can equip them, and then they will make their own way and begin forming their own legacies. This process doesn't begin at eighteen years of age when most leave the house—it's already begun.

My oldest child was at a sleepover party at a "Christian" home. At some point during the evening, the kids began to watch the video, *The Blair Witch Project.* Paris quietly got up from the table, dismissed herself, and went into the kitchen. She didn't preach; she didn't hit anybody over the head with the Bible; she merely walked out of the room. An hour later, eight girls were in the kitchen; two were left watching the movie. Parents, aunts and uncles, and neighbors—we can make a difference. We must encourage others to make good choices.

My son asked me, "You're going to love me no matter what, Mom?"

"Yes, Jordan, no matter what."

"Even if I'm an axe murderer, Mom?"

That boy is such a deep thinker. He's going to turn out normal if it kills me.

I love the sage advice to give children "roots and wings." We are doing our best to give them roots as well as wings so that we may lovingly say, "Go fly." I heard a parable about a man who saw a butterfly about to emerge from a tiny cocoon as he was walking in his garden one day. And as he watched the butterfly struggling to free itself of the cocoon, he noted it was making such slow progress in its cumbersome chore. The man pitied the poor creature and thought about how he could help it along. He grabbed a small pair of scissors and gave the cocoon a little snip at the opening. However, he didn't realize that instead of helping, he had actually hindered the butterfly. God created this seemingly painful and slow birthing process so that the pressure of working against the tightly woven cocoon causes the blood to slowly course through the veins in their wings. Finally, when the blood is fully circulating, the butterfly emerges as a perfectly aerodynamic creature. The man's small snip released the pressure. When that butterfly eventually emerged from its cocoon, it was permanently stunted and could never fly.

I want to encourage those who desire to leave a strong legacy to children. Beware of constantly getting the children you love out of trouble instead of allowing them to face the consequences of their actions. We think we are "helping" our children by getting them out of difficult situations. But when we "snip" them out of tight places—at school, in relationships, or regarding responsibilities—we are potentially cutting off their blood supply so that they will not "fly" like God intended them to fly. They will remain handicapped at many levels.

LEGACIES INVOLVE EVERYTHING WE TOUCH

I hope you're beginning to see that our legacy is so much more than just a biological reproduction of people. Those without children have an equally valuable legacy to leave. We all have a responsibility to the world around us. I can leave a legacy in my neighborhood. I can leave a legacy in my business community. I can leave a legacy in whatever it is that I'm involved with. There's only one me. There's only one you. God wants to use us uniquely in every situation. Think of all the people we come into contact with in our daily routine—the UPS deliverer, the waitress at lunch, the guy who bags your groceries, the office receptionist. You may be the only Christian in that person's life. As the saying goes, "You are the only Bible some people might ever read." God certainly desires for you to touch those in your sphere.

If it's true that a person starts to look like his or her spouse after many years of marriage, imagine how that relates to Christians. We can aspire to "look" like Jesus. Adopting His contagious smile and His welcoming embrace. Growing more patient. Loving others unconditionally. Scripture introduces an exciting proposition when it says that you have "taken off your old self with its practices and have put on the new self, which is being renewed in knowledge in the image of its Creator" (Col. 3:9–10).

When a woman wearing sweet-smelling perfume walks into a room, sometimes other's will ask, "Excuse me, what is that you're wearing?" Something about that woman captures their attention. Wouldn't it be nice if others were curious about our "spiritual scent"? In the same way, the essence of fine Christian men naturally draws coworkers, neighbors, and relatives closer to God through consistent, caring interaction. In fact, the Bible encourages us to have this effect on others.

> But thanks be to God, who always leads us in triumphal procession in Christ and through us spreads everywhere the fragrance of the knowledge of him. For we are to God the aroma of Christ among those who are being saved and those who are perishing. To the one we are the smell of death; to the other, the fragrance of life. (2 Cor. 2:14–16)

At times, we may see a perfect stranger in the airport or at the bookstore, and we just know that person is a Christian. It's just splashing off of him or her and onto others. Unfortunately, some people splash other things besides God's love—unpleasant traits and qualities that repel people instead of attract them. I want people to inhale sweetness in my character, not bitterness or unpleasantness. Matthew 12:35 says, "The good man brings good things out of the good stored up in him, and the evil man brings evil things out of the evil stored up in him." When you start to look like Jesus and smell like Jesus from the inside out, you leave a legacy of a wonderful aroma that makes others wonder, "What is it about you that makes you so special?" So the next time someone is drawn to you and wants to know what you're wearing—you can stand up straight and smile and say "Jesus." They just might inquire more about *Him*—because He smells so good on *you*.

CHAPTER TWELVE

PASSING ON WHAT MATTERS

My son, Jordan, is a very sensitive boy. He says, "I love you," for no reason at all. If I'm in the hallway carrying a stack of newspapers or a basket of laundry, he'll occasionally kiss my forearm as he passes by me. I hope he'll still send some kisses my way when he heads to college. On the other hand, my oldest teenager, Paris, is into her personal space. Some days she comes home from school and greets me with a formal, "Hello, Mother."

"Who's that?" I ask myself. When did I become "Mother"? When I ask Paris for a hug or a kiss, she informs me one is coming soon. Capri, the youngest, is attached to my hip for the most part, but she is also touch and go with affection. I'm considering buying Jordan a new car and the girls can ride bikes to college.

When Jordan was in fourth grade, his teacher invited all the parents for a "holiday gathering." The students had made special "gifts" in the form of decorated essays for the parents which were proudly posted on the bulletin board. All the thin, blonde women were admiring the projects, flipping through them and making all kinds of flattering comments to one another. Oddly, no one was saying anything to me. (At the time, I was pudgy and had very big New York hair.) Oh well, I reached for a brownie and kept reading.

I must admit, I nearly choked up when I spotted Jordan's creation. It was entitled, "A Gift to My Mom." I was so excited. I glanced at the first sentence and paused to pour myself some bug juice in a Dixie cup. I smiled broadly when I read the opening words, "I would like to give a gift to my mom that I cannot buy." I felt my heart skip a beat. What a sweet boy. What a deep soul. So young, and yet he knows the best things in life do not have price tags. My eyes moistened and I continued reading, "I am going to give this gift to my mom because I love her so much, and I think she needs this present." Picture me beaming at this point, just beaming.

The thin blonde women were smiling and nodding, looking over my shoulder, as if to make comparisons. I continued on, "I don't know why she needs this gift. I guess that's just the way it is. She said herself that she would love this wonderful present so I want to give it to her." By now, I'm reading aloud and my eyes are filling up with tears. "The gift that I'm going to give my mom is … " The admiring onlookers waited for me to turn the page in anticipation. " … the gift of … organization." ORGANIZATION??? Uhhhhhhhhhhhhh!

One woman snickered, two walked away, and one tried to air-hug me. Ouch! I returned my gaze toward the bulletin board. "I choose to give this gift to my mom because she's not organized. Mom is messy most of the time. Organization is a very good thing to have. My dad is organized. I hope my mom really likes this gift." I vaguely remember a blonde neighbor patting me sympathetically saying, "It's all right, honey." My eyes were moist once again, but the emotion was different.

Parents, grandparents, aunts, and uncles who have a healthy self-esteem and a love for Jesus would like for children to take after them in some ways. By the same token, if they have made an honest self-assessment, they would also choose for the children *not* to take after them in some ways. After all, we're all working out our salvation in fear and trembling. I'm confident that my kids will get enough organizational aptitude from their father. And I hope to teach them to be tenderhearted and use words effectively and with eternal impact. But I also hope they'll turn to Jesus before they turn to either of us for many character traits.

Romans 8:29 tells us to be conformed to the image of Christ; it does not reference the people we admire most. I'm reminding my kids every day that their father and I are not the ultimate role models. We are conforming to the image of God's Son, Jesus. *He* is the Good News. We can't go wrong emulating Him. I like how Paul put it: "Follow my example as I follow the example of Christ" (1 Cor. 11:1).

As I try to follow Christ's example, I want to pass on to others what matters most. When Grandma Mannarino died, the family got the meatball recipe, and it's valuable. There were also special pieces of jewelry, furniture, and property. Like the stones Israel gathered to build a memorial for future generations, what we pass on to others comes in all shapes and sizes. I want to return to that image of the Israelites scouring the river bottom trying to find twelve perfect stones (one for each of the twelve tribes). I've identified a few stones of my own that can be used to form an enduring legacy—our own testaments to what matters most in life.

Although many references in the remainder of this chapter relate to children, a legacy is left to anyone we invest in. Of course, I wish to leave a godly legacy to my children, but that's only the starting point. With or without children, *every* believer needs to take this duty and privilege seriously.

STONE ONE: PASS ON ENCOURAGEMENT

It was 1984 and President Ronald Reagan had signed the Equal Access Act—ensuring that all non-school related organizations would have the right to meet on school property without fear of discrimination. Separation of church and state had been widely (and *wildly*) misinterpreted and abuse abounded. I was most familiar with the misinterpretations as they affected the public school arena. Allow me to describe a few actual scenarios in my region. Some students were told not to carry Bibles into their school. Others were told to remove religious jewelry or shirts that were religious in nature. In certain elementary schools, children were told not to talk about, write about, or draw anything related to God. (Out of respect to others.) During the holidays, snowflakes, sleigh bells and Santa were permissible, but references to Jesus Christ at Christmas were taboo. However, references to the Menorah at Hanukkah and to the foundations of Kwanza and Ramadan were politically correct and often welcome. In an affluent Long Island high school, a young lady received a serious threat and legal warnings for establishing a weekly Bible study on school grounds. Several efforts to organize prayer meetings before or after school hours were denied in various school districts but in these same schools groups that convened to learn about Yoga, Transcendental Meditation, and Self Discovery were welcomed. Though the President's bill was passed with great support, there was still much resistance and—might I boldly add—ignorance. The Lamb's Chapel, a small church on eastern Long Island, was denied the use of a nearby school auditorium to show a video series produced by Focus on the Family. Thanks to the diligence of fine Christian attorneys, like my friend Joe Infranco, that case went all the way to the U.S. Supreme Court. They stood for what was right—and they won.

After the ruling, a talented art student approached me about starting a Christian club at William Floyd High School. The law stated that the gathering would have to be initiated, organized, and directed by students. This would deter the abuse of cults or self-promoted "prophets." A stipulation within the law mandated that an adult from the school staff had to be present, for custodial and legal purposes. I was busy getting accustomed to married life, pursuing a master's degree, leading the high school girls at church youth group, and coaching the cheerleaders and ... oh, don't we *always* have a dozen excuses?

After a few planning sessions conducted at a local diner, Floyd Fellowship was born. The kids lined up great speakers, created cool posters and flyers, and brought lots of junk food for the kick-off. Dr. Eric Waxman, the principal, was so supportive that he announced the first meeting of Floyd Fellowship along with the other after-school events over the PA system. I was thrilled. Some of my colleagues were *not*.

Attendance at the meetings vacillated each week. Sometimes fourteen kids, sometimes five, sometimes twenty. Besides the founder, Joe Armeda, and me, one other person showed up every single week, without fail. His name was Andy Fiormante. He wore blue jeans, work boots, a utility belt, and a broad smile. He was a man's man and he had a deep love for Jesus. He sat through every meeting and usually said one or maybe two sentences before we closed with a prayer. There were certain gatherings where he never spoke a word, except to greet the kids as they entered the room, and to make newcomers feel welcomed.

Being the Sponsor of Floyd Fellowship had its price. Certain teachers were appalled that such things could take place on public property. Some felt I had blurred the lines. Others were convinced I was inappropriately proselytizing minors. God knew I needed encouragement. I grew weary at times and came very close to stepping down. Did I mention being a Capital "C" Christian is hard?

Within six months, the kids organized a Christian rock concert to be held in the auditorium. The critics came out of the pea green cinderblocks! But so did the supporters. Walter Myers, the Head Custodian. Gerrie Weiss, the Switchboard Operator. Fellow teachers like Tricia Radican, Bob Peters, and Giovanna Morabito. Richard Lewis, the Assistant Principal, and the beloved Gerri Riker—who served the English

Department (and me) with excellence. She was my prayer warrior from the day I set foot in her small cubicle to meet with the Chairman for an interview.

The dad who I mentioned, Andy Fiormante, did one *more* thing besides attending the meetings of Floyd Fellowship. Every so often, he left a small card on my desk on his way out the door. Reflective of his spoken words at the meetings, his written words were few and powerful. He always included a Bible verse, and he always mentioned what a difference I was making in the lives of the kids. I saved those cards and I took them out of a box on many occasions when I no longer wanted to spend myself. I was so grateful for the Christians in the building who poured encouraging words over me from time to time. And I am so grateful God sent a big man with a big heart to quietly cheer me on as I ran the race in that season of my journey.

"Remember those who led you, who spoke the word of God to you; and considering the result of their conduct, imitate their faith" (Heb. 13:7 NASB).

Those of us who are a bit more seasoned know that the opposite of encouragement has taken place in too many lives. A bruised heart, a shattered dream, and self-loathing are often the results. It's called discouragement. Somebody took away the grand vision and smashed it. Somebody threw cold water on the flame of hope. No one believed in you and you stopped believing as well. But Jesus wants you to have your dream. He does not mind high hopes and large goals. Scripture is filled with people who achieved great things for God. Recapture your worth within the context of being His beloved child and help do the same for others. After all, to encourage simply means "to give someone courage" and Lord knows we all need more of that in this uncertain world. "The tongue has the power of life and death" (Prov. 18:21). What a joy it is to speak life into the spirit of another! Be generous with encouraging words and don't grow weary of handing them out like fragrant flowers. When we give others hope, we are pointing them to the embodiment of hope: Jesus Christ. What a privilege!

The story is told of a group of frogs that was hopping down a dirt road toward the lake when three of the frogs in front fell into a deep hole. The poor frogs jumped and clamored toward the top of the hole, but it was no use. It began to rain and the more the fallen frogs jumped, the more mud they pulled down on themselves. They were sinking deeper and deeper into the thick mud. The other frogs around the edge of the hole became despondent as they watched the futile and exasperated efforts by the three mud-covered frogs. They began screaming into the hole, "Stop! Stop! Forget it. Give up. You're not going to make it! It's no good. Give up!"

Eventually, two of the frogs *did* stop trying. They sank into the mud and suffocated. But one frog kept jumping, straining to get out. He kept jumping and scratching and swallowing mud until he finally made it out of the hole. The other frogs gathered around the lone survivor and asked, "Why did you keep jumping when we told you to quit? What made you keep trying?" Surprised and saddened, the frog looked intently at them and sadly replied, "I'm partially deaf. I couldn't hear you. I thought you were encouraging me. I thought you were cheering me on and telling me I could make it."

The power of our words is the catalyst behind our legacy. It's the engine of the inheritance we leave to others. That little thing that wags in our mouth does a lot of good or a lot of damage. "Likewise the tongue is a small part of the body, but it makes great boasts. Consider what a great forest is set on fire by a small spark" (James 3:5).

A friend of mine who is a Christian psychologist likes to say, "Hurt people hurt people. Healed people heal people." Sticks and stones haven't ever been thrown my way, but I do have painful memories of being hit hard by words. Words can hurt and words can heal; I have used words with both outcomes in mind. Oh, how I long to gain full control of my words! More accurately, how I yearn to give full control of my tongue to the Holy Spirit. Self-control is a sweet fruit of the spirit that we need to nurture if we are going to pass on encouraging words.

STONE TWO: PASS ON AN AWARENESS OF GIFTS AND CAPABILITIES

Child psychologist and family expert Dr. James Dobson says if parents are raising all their children alike, they're making a big mistake. Children have individual temperaments, and we need to pass on the tools they need to recognize and use their gifts and capabilities. What one child excels in may not be true for the other child.

Ladybird Johnson once said that "our children become what we call them." If a child is told long enough, "You can't do it. You're not going to make it. You're never going to be such and such," that child is more than likely going to fail in his or her pursuits. Many often abort a mission or long-term goal before they ever begin. Psychologists have a fancy term for it: "negative self-fulfilling prophecy." Self-fulfilling prophecies occur when people draw conclusions about themselves from repeated words and then act as if those conclusions were true. In other words, they act in such a way as to make the conclusion "come true."

Some people hit a premature developmental ceiling because they feel nobody believes in them. Conversely, what if we're told, "You're a winner, and you can achieve whatever you want to"? I tell my daughters, "If you want to be a dancer, lawyer, baker, or doctor, you *can,* honey ... and you *will.*" I meet so many young girls who have low self-esteem, and yet there are those who feel that they'll be the first female president or the first woman on the moon. How does that happen? What is making the difference? The answer is not a "what," but rather a "who." Somebody is speaking words of affirmation and encouragement into that life.

Everyone wants to know, "What am I good at?" We hear too often about the areas in which we don't meet someone's expectations. How about building someone up with something you noticed that's positive and affirming? Have you observed coaches or teachers who do that regularly? It's grace in motion and it's very attractive. Children (large and small) need us to be at their sides more than they need us on their backs.

The workplace is an ideal place to begin encouraging people in their gifts and capabilities. Instead of adding your two cents to the cubicle gossip about who's a pain, have a positive word. Speak to people about their gifts more than their shortcomings and you'll notice a change. People's performance will improve when they know someone cares about them. You can read that in any best-selling motivational manual. Those who encourage us and tell us that we're special and show their appreciation are those we go out of our way to please.

STONE THREE: PASS ON WHAT YOU VALUE

When Frank worked with Prison Fellowship International, he traveled to prisons in the most remote places inside third world countries. Somehow I never felt led to accompany him on *those* trips. However, when he had board meetings in Paris and London, I felt a deep need to go and be supportive. *Lord, forgive me.*

Paris went with Frank to a prison in Ecuador when she was ten years old. Frank arranged for twelve doctors and three dentists to work twelve hours a day for a week to pull and stitch and cut. Paris was horrified that first day. By the second day, she was filling hypodermic needles and handing them to the doctors. I love that she had an indelible experience ministering to others alongside her father. Jordan had similar experiences in several African countries. I often tell parents, "If your kids are spoiled complainers, take them on a field trip." You may not be able to go to Ecuador or

Zimbabwe, but take them to a shelter or a nursing home or a food distribution center—a place where they can interact with those who are less fortunate or lonely or in need of a hug and a smile.

The Gospel Rescue Mission is in downtown Washington, D.C., and we went there one Thanksgiving to spend the day preparing and serving turkey dinner. Everyone pitched in. I had made plans to go to a lovely restaurant later that night to enjoy our "own" Thanksgiving dinner. After serving dozens of stuffed turkeys and mountains of potatoes and gravy all day, my family unanimously voted for Chinese take-out and a video instead. I felt an insurgence of "mother knows best" instincts rise within me. I wanted them to have the perfect Thanksgiving. We would serve the poor and then *we* would be served. They all groaned and presented their cases. Just when I was about to launch my defense, Capri (who was eight at the time) passionately blurted, "Mommy, we already *had* Thanksgiving." She got it. My family got it. I was the only one who didn't get it. I am so glad God is patient and kind.

I've heard that a person's checkbook will reveal what he or she truly values. That said, our personal planners reveal where we are spending our *most* valuable resource: our time. What is on the calendar in the coming months that demonstrates your commitment to serve others? Like many others, I would much rather give money than my time, but what am I modeling if my giving is solely monetary? Financial giving is important and scripturally sound, but we must also "tithe our time" to institutions and worthy causes. How can I say "I love my neighbors" if I only wave at them? Sending rice to an orphanage and placing a spoon of rice into an orphan's mouth are two very different experiences. The former makes one more holy. The latter makes one more whole. Besides the Triune God, only two other things are eternal—His Word and our souls. They alone last forever. We must invest our lives in these two things. They are where we will find value.

Jordan, (my sensitive son), had to make a family crest for a school project when he was seven. The teacher pre-cut beautifully shaped crests with four quadrants. Each quadrant was supposed to represent one member of the family. Jordan put a plane on Frank's quadrant since Frank was flying so much for the work of Prison Fellowship International. He named the plane, "mishenerry plane." I was so proud. It was misspelled, but so sweet. Next, he had big sister Paris as a courageous lioness—strong and powerful. At the time, Capri was just a baby, so Jordan put himself in the third quadrant— a bold and daring dragon. In the final quadrant was a picture of a fat bear sleeping.

I asked, in a raised tone, "Jordan, *what* is that?"

"It's a Mommy Bear."

"Why am I sleeping?"

"Oh, Mom, you *love* to take naps."

At least it wasn't hung on a bulletin board. *Humble yourself in the sight of the Lord or your children will do it for you.*

What is important to you? What do you value above all else? If you're not sure or it's a close tie between a few things, ask those who know you well what *they* think is important to you. Their answers may be a bit unsettling. What would you choose to hang in the entrance of your home that boldly announces to every visitor what you esteem most? The biblical hero, Joshua, said "Choose for yourself this day whom you will serve ... But as for me and my household, we will serve the Lord" (Josh. 24:15).

When we place a high priority on caring for the needs of others, then what the Bible teaches about putting others' needs before our own becomes relevant. When we truly reach out to others—over a meal or on a mission trip, the impact on our home is exciting. What Jesus teaches about "giving" being better than "taking" suddenly has new meaning. Some of the fondest memories I have are of the times when Frank brought home guests we had never met to join us for supper. "Do not forget to entertain strangers, for by so doing some people have entertained angels without knowing it" (Heb. 13:2).

Stone Four: Pass on a Priority on God's Word

I am a photo-crazy person. Those who know me well can attest to the fact that I contribute to the profit margin of Kodak. Every year I tell myself that I will take all the negatives out of the house and place them in a fireproof safe. I know people now have their photos on disk, but, please, let's not get into that. Frank and I still haven't figured out how to record from the TV to the VCR so we're not quite ready for the big switch to digital. Someday ...

While we often place a high value on things like photos, gadgets, or other tangible treasures, we need to approach spiritual things with enthusiasm as well. When we place a high value on God's Word, we are not adding value to it. It's valuable on its own. We simply acknowledge its worth. We don't need to thump anyone on the head with a Bible, but we do need to allow our family, our coworkers, and our friends to see its place in our lives. I want my kids to see their mom reading the Bible and living it out. I want those who know me to recognize the prominent place God's Word has in my life. I don't want to be apologetic or reticent when it comes to such things.

If we want to pass on what matters, we let others see the valuable role our faith plays in our daily lives. I seek the same few cashiers at the supermarket checkout line nearly every time I shop. After almost ten years of interacting with them as they scan my items, I have discovered I can share God's love five or ten minutes at a time. Do my efforts to share His Word make a difference? Absolutely!

Whenever I asked Shelley how she was or what was new, she would invariably complain about what a "sorry excuse for a husband" she married. Divorce seemed inevitable. There were lots of encounters where she did the talking and I did the listening. When I finally earned the right to speak, I was able to share about the One who heals, restores, and rescues. She was listening. Imagine my deep joy when she recently shouted across a few lanes: "Hey, we went to church last week and I'm gonna stay married!"

> As the rain and the snow
>   come down from heaven,
> and do not return to it

> without watering the earth
> and making it bud and flourish,
>   so that it yields seed for the sower
>   and bread for the eater,
> so is my word that goes out from
>   my mouth:
> It will not return to me empty,
> but will accomplish what I desire
>   and achieve the purpose for which I
>   sent it.
>   (Isa. 55:10–11)

Likewise, I encourage my kids to share their faith with their peers at school. It is not an easy task. When our oldest daughter was a sophomore at Herndon High School, a classmate whom she chatted with daily came up to her between classes and said, "Paris, I just want you to know that you ruined Saturday night." Paris was stunned. What was she talking about? The sixteen-year-old continued, "I was going to have sex with my boyfriend, and I *didn't* because I thought of *you!*" I finally convinced Paris to take it as a compliment. And it truly was. How I wish my Christian witness in high school was as deep and strong as my daughter's is.

STONE FIVE: PASS ON WISDOM FROM LIFE'S EXPERIENCES

Someone said parenthood is the only work where once you're qualified, you no longer have a job. One of the things I miss the most about New York is the brownstones and row houses. Grandma or Aunt Mary lived upstairs, downstairs, or next door—there was plenty of parenting advice and never any need to hunt for baby-sitters. In New York, I had backups for my backup baby-sitters. There were plenty of generous offers to watch the kids for a night or a week. I really miss that. But what I miss most is "stoops".

In Brooklyn, houses have stoops. In simplest terms, a stoop is a row of cement or brick steps leading to the front door where there is a small landing. My friends in the deep south fondly refer to their porches. Porches are made of wood and they're much larger than stoops. The fun thing about stoops is that you have to step carefully over people and climb a few steps and squeeze your behind in to claim a spot. There are no stoops in my neighborhood here in Virginia. No sir. No place for cousins, aunts, grandmothers, and mothers to congregate in the cool of the day after the laundry was done, the dinner was started, and the babies were put down for a nap. In the old neighborhood, family and friends would carry each other's babies as well as their burdens. No fuss. No airs. No need to impress. People would shout next door or across the street, "Come by for coffee and a piece of cake! I'll put on a pot." The stoop was a place where life made sense. At dusk, we'd catch fireflies in empty baby food jars that had a couple of holes in the lid, thanks to whoever had a hammer and nail handy.

On or near the stoop, adults solved the problems of the world and children waited for the Bungalow Bar Man or Mr. Softee to drive down the street. The more seasoned citizens would share their wisdom on a variety of subjects that should be required reading before becoming an adult. If you listened carefully, you could pick up all kinds of helpful tips about what to expect during the early years of marriage or how to raise kids who turn out all right. After having a first fight as newlyweds or experiencing a lay-off at work—it helped to hear someone else had gone through the same thing and survived. Sometimes just hearing the words, "This too shall pass" was enough to know everything was going to be okay. It was their version of psychotherapy. And it was free. Now you pay a lot of money to a stranger who will *not* come to your house and who will *definitely* not hold your baby! I miss stoops.

I'm convinced that one of the contributors to depression and other forms of mental suffering is loneliness and loss of human interaction. We are becoming isolated. We click the remote control on the garage to venture out, and at the end of the day, *click,* we go right back in the way we came. I haven't used my front door key in years. We lay our cell phones on the table when we eat, and we have sadly tolerated the constant interruptions. We spend hours with the computer monitor, and we have lost the art of communication. It's so easy to seal ourselves off from others and it's so dangerous. When we rarely or never interact with others at a significant level—significant enough to find out what's *really* going on in each other's lives—we can begin to believe the lie that we are the only ones struggling with problems.

In Brooklyn, when you had a disagreement about finances with your spouse or the baby had a strange rash, you had "local experts" to tell you, "It's okay, it's normal." Today, many marriages go through typical stages of ebb and flow without the benefit of feedback. It's easy for couples to assume they must be headed for divorce court when they think they're the only ones with problems. Having someone who's "been there, done that" to talk to about our problems can help us step back and look at the big picture. One of the key roles we can play with friends, neighbors, and colleagues is to be that reasonable and wise person who will help put things in perspective for others.

Do you want to leave a godly legacy? Then pass on the tools others need to grow into their God-given potential. This idea of learning from each other is modeled throughout Scripture. The apostle Paul, when writing to Timothy, encouraged him to put into practice what others had taught him. Paul pointed to his own forefathers in the faith (2 Tim. 1:3) and encouraged Timothy to follow the spiritual example of his mother and grandmother. "I have been reminded of your sincere faith, which first lived in your grandmother Lois and in your mother Eunice and, I am persuaded, now lives in you also" (2 Tim. 1:5). What a legacy!

I was single during the first ten years of being a follower of Jesus. Christian families from church invited me for dinner when I was a teen, and terrific women welcomed me into their homes in my early twenties. As a first-generation Christian, I didn't know what Capital "C" Christians *did* at dinnertime. I didn't know how Christian couples disagreed. I didn't know how Christian parents talked to kids. These godly ladies let me in their homes and their hearts. I hung around on weekends and for home groups. I watched. I took notes. And I learned so much.

Today more than ever, the Sanka generation needs to invite the Starbucks generation into their homes and share from their experiences. Most of us can come up with plenty of reasons *not* to invite people over. The gift of hospitality is in danger of extinction! Don't let it happen. When you are committed to God's purpose for your life, every day becomes a new opportunity to make a difference in *other* people's lives. The life poured out is the life God fills.

WHAT DO THESE STONES MEAN?

The stones I pass on may not be as widely visible as the stones Israel gathered for a memorial to future generations, but they serve as an enduring reminder—a testament to the leap of faith *I* have made by trusting in a loving God. Though none can know the future, I have *every* hope and intention of leaving a legacy that includes an enduring marriage. It's a serious contract and I plan to see it through. My parents were divorced after twenty-six "above average" years. As a couple, they were smart, sophisticated, nice to know and beautiful to behold. Obviously, that wasn't enough. God was an incidental ingredient—not a driving force. He is the strong chord that ties me to Frank.

I have every hope and intention of leaving a legacy that includes three fine human beings named Paris, Jordan, and Capri. Parenting brings unspeakable joy but it can be brutal at times. It's hard work and it's not for the lazy, the selfish, or the weak. Though they will choose their own paths, I am warmed and encouraged by the good fruit I see growing from good soil. God is not a stranger to them. He is the centerpiece of our home.

I have every hope and intention of leaving a legacy that includes a hearty response to the commandment to love my neighbors. Though I often fall short, I press in to lend a hand, bring a meal, offer an ear, or just be the first to wave. Little things matter. And I am passionate about impacting my community. I *know* how to live forever, how to heal a marriage, how to get a broken heart mended, how to find lasting joy and irrepressible hope, and how to laugh at the days to come. *I should keep it all to myself?* If I don't speak up, the trees will shout out, the mountains will come forth and I'll burst! No way! I'm going to heaven and I'm taking as many people as I can along with me. It's a wonderful life.

On the night before he was murdered by rebels, a Christian pastor in an African village penned these words:

I am part of the "Fellowship of the
Unashamed." I have Holy Spirit power. The die
has been cast. I've stepped over the line. The
decision has been made. I am a disciple of His.
I won't look back, let up, slow down, back
away, or be still. My past is redeemed, my
present makes sense, and my future is secure. I
am finished and done with low living, sight
walking, small planning, smooth knees, color-
less dreams, tame visions, mundane talking,
chintzy giving, and dwarfed goals!
I no longer need preeminence, prosperity,

position, promotions, plaudits, or popularity. I
don't have to be right, first, tops, recognized,
praised, regarded, or rewarded. I now live by
presence, lean by faith, love by patience, lift
by prayer, and labor by power.

My face is set, my gait is fast, my goal is
heaven, my road is narrow, my way is rough,
my companions few, my Guide reliable, my
mission clear. I cannot be bought, compromised, detoured, lured away, turned away,
turned back, diluted, or delayed. I will not
flinch in the face of sacrifice, hesitate in the
presence of adversity, negotiate at the table of
the enemy, ponder at the pool of popularity,
or meander in the maze of mediocrity.

I won't give up, shut up, let up, or burn up
till I've preached up, prayed up, paid up, stored
up, and stayed up for the cause of Christ.

I am a disciple of Jesus. I must go till He
comes, give till I drop, preach till all know,
and work till He stops.

And when he comes to get His own, He'll
have no problems recognizing me. My colors
will be clear.[10]

*Oh Lord, give me THAT kind of resolve! I want to leave a legacy
that will please you. I want my colors to be bold and pure and eternal. Help me Lord ... how I need you.*

I know that there will come a day when I take my ultimate, final leap of faith. The final leap of faith is the one we take from this life to the next. For the Christian, it's the ultimate leap toward our final reward—a place called heaven. The final leap of faith is not a cruel or mindless long jump into some dark abyss. In fact, Scripture tells us a great deal about heaven:

We will have an eternal house.

We will have citizenship.

We will have our names written in the Book of Life.

We will receive every blessing.

We will attend the wedding supper of the Lamb.

We will sing a new song.

We will have our tears wiped away.

We will see no more death or crying or pain.

We will see God face to face.

We will worship God forever.

We will reign with God forever.

I will go there someday.

It won't be a day of my own choosing, but when it comes I will take the leap toward *that* life with peace and confidence. And I will spend the rest of *this* life encouraging others to come along.

An Invitation

You may have picked up this book because you've attended a retreat or conference or maybe a trusted friend or family member said to give it a try. By this point you have gotten to know me a little. But more importantly, I hope you have gotten to know the God I worship. If we were sharing a short chat or a meal together, I would sincerely ask you about your life—about what you believe and who or what brings you hope and joy each day.

So … how are you? How are things going? Where are you in your spiritual journey?

What has been robbing you of your peace? Maybe you have never seen Jesus as being real, alive, relevant, or intimate. Or maybe you have known Him but right now He seems very far away—He's not—He loves you. Come home … He has kept the light on and He is waiting for you. No condemnation. Just open arms. Take the leap of faith toward Him.

Dear friend, He was born for us, He died for us, and He rose to give us eternal life. He wants to bring hope to each and every human being. He longs to be invited in:

> "Here I am!" Jesus says, "I stand at the door [of your heart] and knock. If anyone hears my voice and opens the door, I will come in and eat with him, and he with me" (Rev. 3:20).

Pray this simple prayer right now …

> *Lord Jesus, I know I have sinned in my thoughts, words, and actions. I'm sorry. I don't want to live that way anymore. I ask You to come into my life. Be my advocate and forgive me. Be my Savior and cleanse me. Be my Lord and guide me. You are the giver of life—I humbly give my life back to You. Amen.*

If you still have questions, check out www.GrowinginChrist.com

EPILOGUE

I especially love the company of women, and it is a great joy to meet so many unsung heroes along life's way. After retreats, it's sometimes hard to say goodbye. I'm so glad we'll all have a few billion years to catch up on things later. A particularly difficult goodbye was the one I exchanged with Kara Nadeau on the Sunday afternoon of that memorable weekend in New Jersey. The women's committee had invited me to return exactly five months later to speak at a full day conference, to be held in the church sanctuary. On the Sunday afternoon of that fall retreat, as everyone hugged and filed out, I gave extra tight hugs to Kara and her family. We had certainly connected in a special way. With smiles and tears, Kara leaned her face toward mine and told me her goal was to "be there" for the spring conference. Her family agreed it was a good goal.

Kara died just three weeks before the conference. I had the privilege of talking with her and with Annie a couple of times before she went to heaven. On March 12, 2003, Peggy, from the women's committee, sent a two-word e-mail: *"She's home!"* I *know* she is. I was unable to attend the funeral because of a speaking commitment, but I am told that Kara's three sisters stood to testify about Kara's gift of faith to each of them.

The day of the spring conference came and I was pleased to see some faces from the retreat where we met five months earlier. I was to speak three times that day. In the middle of the first session, I said something funny. It was *very* funny (if I may say so myself) and I enjoyed surveying the faces and body language across the large sanctuary. I happened to glance toward the far left section and there, a third of the way back, were Kara's mom and her sister Annie, laughing just as hard as the others. My words kept flowing but my heart skipped a beat as I had a few fleeting thoughts. *They live in Massachusetts. They just buried Kara three weeks ago. They're here at a Christian women's conference. They are listening and learning and laughing. Thank you Lord for the healing gift of laughter. Help me say what you want, Lord. Help me share what they need to hear.*

The session ended in prayer and I made a beeline off the platform and toward the two precious women. We embraced and I could not hold back my tears. *Would I be at a large church gathering three weeks after burying my child? Lord give me that faith.* They had come to help Kara's husband, David, with closets and drawers. They had come to be with those sweet little boys. They had come to feel near to Kara. Pat Donohue looked a bit weary. "Kara *really* wanted to be here today. So we came *for* her."

The day flew by, as they always do and I closed the conference with an invitation to receive Jesus as Lord or to recommit to His Lordship. Women flowed forward as worship music played gently and prayers were lifted. I prayed with several women and turned at one point to find Kara's mom behind me. We locked hands. Annie was at her side, trickling tears of joy. Pat squeezed my hands tightly, "I was dreading coming back here, but I really needed this day. This is exactly where God wanted me to be. I've been religious all my life but I haven't been a Capital "C" Christian. I *know* Kara is in heaven. I want to know Jesus like *she* knew Jesus."

I want that for Pat, and for her daughters, and for everyone whose life was touched by Kara. And I want that for *you*, too. I know Kara took a leap of faith many, many times in her life. A leap into a relationship with Jesus, though her contemporaries were leaping toward other things. A leap into marriage and motherhood and giving up position, plaudits and power to stay home with leaky diapers. A leap into enemy territory called cancer. A leap to love and believe in God though no relief came. A leap to speak of the joy He provides in the midst of pain and suffering. A leap to trust God with the care of her precious husband and two little boys. A leap to invite others to meet her in heaven, even during her last days on earth.

But Kara's final leap of faith was also her ultimate reward—to be gathered into the strong arms of our loving God, with whom she will spend eternity. I've learned so much from the vibrant woman who took her family on a life-giving retreat in the midst of her dying process. I have addressed thousands of women since I met Kara and I happily share her story. Many have come into a deeper relationship with God because of her.

Kara lives. Now that's a legacy.

KARA DONOHUE NADEAU

KARA'S MOM (PAT) AND SISTER (ANNIE)

YOUR OWN LEAP OF FAITH

A STUDY GUIDE
FOR
PERSONAL REFLECTION
AND DISCUSSION

Sometimes it feels as if life just *happens*. We get caught up in the details of our everyday existence, moving from one distraction to the next without really *living*. There is always one more unfinished project to complete, one more errand to run, one more newspaper to read, ... indeed, one more load of laundry to wash.

The subtitle of this book is not *"Settling for the Life You've Got"*, but rather *"Embracing the Life God Promised"* We have observed in the pages herein that each leap of faith we take is by a conscious decision to trust in our loving and faithful God. By taking a leap of faith, we can overcome those very things that would have sidelined or derailed us in a life apart from Him.

The following study guide is intended to help you examine your own life in the areas covered in this book—your fears, your desires, your heritage, your legacy—so that you, too, will be prepared and *excited* to take a leap of faith when it is warranted.

The questions in the study guide have been designed for use by individuals or by groups. Use this guide during personal devotions. Or use it in a small group book study. However you utilize this study, may you grow closer to our loving and almighty Father.

CHAPTER ONE

CAPITAL "C" CHRISTIAN

Ellie describes her family and the typical Sunday meal rit-
uals. She says, "There was an awareness of the *existence*
of God—but not the experience of God. Religion came
up from time to time, but there wasn't much discussion—other than ours was right and everyone else's was
wrong." What was your family like? Was religion discussed openly? What kinds of discussions did you have?

Do you tend to declare your faith to be "personal," or are
you more likely to "go and tell"?

How would you define or describe a Capital "C" Christian?
Who around you would you label a Capital "C"
Christian? Are you one? Why or why not?

Ellie describes how our "first love" enthusiasm will often dwindle to the point where "our Christian pulse is barely detectable." Have you experienced this? Describe your "first love" enthusiasm and what you are currently experiencing.

Ellie writes, "Christians are not immune to trouble, but we are equipped to respond differently than those without relationship with the Savior." Have you had a tragedy since becoming a Christian? Describe how your response is different than it would have been without a relationship with Christ.

Matthew 7:21 says, "Not everyone who says to me, 'Lord, Lord, will enter the kingdom of heaven, but only he who does the will of my Father who is in heaven." How does this Scripture relate to Capital "C" Christians?

TAKE THE LEAP

Do you live as a child of the King, or more like a spiritual pauper? What is keeping you from claiming the abundant life God offers?

What are some of the "membership privileges" of Christianity?

This chapter includes the story of Alexander, the boy who rode in steerage despite having a first class ticket for his journey. Ellie says, "Aren't we a bit like Alexander? ... We are content with much less than He planned for us. We crane our necks and look at other people's lives and we stare and make wishes and fantasize." How have you been like Alexander? How can you fully utilize your "first class ticket"?

Why are people so drawn in to media "empresses" such as Oprah Winfrey? What are they really seeking? Will they find what they are looking for here? If not, where can they find solutions?

Colossians 2:9–10 says, "For in Christ all the fullness of the Deity lives in bodily form, and you have been given fullness in Christ, who is the head over every power and authority." Does your daily life reflect this promise? How does this Scripture confirm that we, as Christians, have been given a "first class ticket"?

CHAPTER THREE

DESTINED FOR MORE

Ellie describes her unwanted move from the comforts of
New York into the unknown land of Virginia and the
subsequent life-changing ministry of Prison Fellowship.
Has God ever called you out of a comfortable, familiar
lifestyle into something else? What did you feel? How did
you respond? What was the outcome?

The woman in prison wrote a letter about how she wasted
so much of her time waiting, thinking some day life
would begin when "this or that happened." Has your
good life really begun, or are you still waiting? What are
you "waiting until"?

What sequence of events has happened in your life that you
can look back on and see God's hand in?

Ellie's mission statement is "To know Him and make Him known." What is your personal mission statement? What are you here for?

A.W. Tozer asks, "What comes into your mind when you think about God is the most important thing about you." Describe your image of God. What is He like?

While in prison Paul said, "And of this gospel I was appointed a herald and an apostle and a teacher. That is why I am suffering as I am. Yet I am not ashamed, because I know whom I have believed, and am convinced that he is able to guard what I have entrusted to him for that day" (2 Tim. 1:11–12). Paul carried on his ministry wherever he was, despite all physical hardships. What kept him going? What can you learn from Paul as you encounter difficulties in your life? What does this Scripture teach you about being useful to God wherever you live?

CHAPTER FOUR

GOD'S PROMISES

"I will give you this land" ... Has God been telling you He wants to give you some new territory—some new place you have yet to see in your spiritual life? What "land" around you is ripe for the harvest? (Relationships at home? In your office? In your community?)

"I will make your name great" ... So often we convince ourselves that greatness is for others: athletes, movie stars, political heroes, successful businessmen, popular evangelists. Why don't we see greatness in ourselves? What roles do you lead in your everyday life in which you can strive for greatness (friend, daughter, son, spouse, teacher, small group leader, painter, etc.)? What is one way you can strive for greatness in each of the roles you list?

"I will bless you ... and you will be a blessing" ... How has God blessed you over your lifetime (friends, family, job,

etc.)? When did you last express your gratitude to Him for these blessings? Spend some time right now in prayer, thanking God for all of the riches—seen and unseen—that He has bestowed upon you.

"I will make you into a great nation" ... Ellie says in this chapter, "It is so exciting to have the privilege to present the good news of God's promise to others. God has promised you people—are you taking Him up on the promise?" What people do you have regular contact with (coworkers, fellow soccer moms, classmates, neighbors)? How can you present God's promise to these people?

Romans 4:16 says, "Therefore, the promise comes by faith, so that it may be by grace and may be guaranteed to all Abraham's offspring—not only to those who are of the law but also to those who are of the faith of Abraham. He is the father of all of us." What reassurances can you find in this verse (and throughout Romans 4)? What do you have to do to receive God's promise?

CHAPTER FIVE

FROM FEAR TO FAITH

Kara, the remarkable woman dying of cancer, shared the secret of her acceptance of suffering: "You can't pin your hopes on living." Why do we so often "pin our hopes on living"? Aside from faith in God, where else do we tend to pin our hopes?

Have you ever had an experience that caused you to question your faith? What was the outcome?

What "hopeless" situations have you experienced where your faith has sustained you? Can you see how the hand of God worked through that situation?

Ellie explains that "fear the Lord" is meant to translate "be in awe of the Lord" rather than "be afraid of the Lord". How does this translation change your interpretation of verses containing the phrase "fear the Lord"?

Ellie says, "If we are honest with ourselves, we may be afraid of what God is going to ask us to do, so we choose to go our own way instead." When have you been afraid of what God might ask you to do? Describe the situation, the choices you made, and the outcome. Now think about how the situation might have been different if you had chosen your way instead of God's (or God's way instead of your own).

Psalm 27:1 says, "The Lord is my light and my salvation—whom shall I fear? The Lord is the stronghold of my life—of whom shall I be afraid?" What reassurances does this Scripture give you? How can we conquer fear?

CHAPTER SIX

LEAVING THE SANDS OF CERTAINTY

This chapter includes a quote from a woman, Barbara, who said, "I don't have joy *because* of the problem; I have joy in the *midst* of the problem." Can you think of a situation in your own life where you can thank God for what He is going to do?

"Before the remaining Israelites could enter the Promised Land, they had to forge a river of impossibility ... . Our own river of impossibility is anything that stands in the way of our receiving God's promises." What is your own personal river of impossibility? What is it about your future that has you afraid to leave the shores of certainty and security? What or who are you afraid to leave behind?

"God assured Joshua, 'You will know which way to go ... ' When our footsteps falter as we contemplate the deep waters of our river of impossibility, God says, 'Follow me.

237

Then you will know which way to go. You will know how to act and what to say in order to overcome.'" Think of a situation in your life where you "don't know which way to go." What should you do?

At the end of this chapter, Ellie talks about being "between trapezes"—hovering between the known and the unknown. Why is it so hard to let go of the "known" and take the leap of faith to the "unknown"? Are you currently holding onto any "known" trapezes—ones where you continue to swing only in the past? What will it take for you to "let go"?

Read Matthew 14: 22–33. In what way does Peter model his trust in Jesus by "stepping out" into uncertainty? What happens when Peter takes his eyes off of Jesus? What saves him? What does this story teach you about trusting Jesus as you walk through your own tough situations and adversity?

CHAPTER SEVEN

WHAT NOW?

Are you allowing destructive, unedifying influences to enter your home through television, computers, music, movies, magazines, or maybe books? How can you adjust your habits and choices to align them more with God's will?

Do you find it hard to share your Christian views because you are afraid of what others might think of you? Explain.

Ellie writes, "We blame others, but we don't want to be blamed. *Well, you don't understand. I'm like this because of my mother. You should see my family, and that would explain me. You should have been around when my father lost his temper.*" Are there areas of your life in which you blame others for your attitudes or actions? Explain.

How does being "set apart" differ from being "separatist"?
Are there areas of your life that could be classified as
"separatist"? In what ways are you "set apart"?

Does your church or ministry readily welcome newcomers?
Even if the newcomers don't "look like us or smell like us
or talk like us or walk like us"?

Paul said, "I am not ashamed of the gospel, because it is
the power of God for the salvation of everyone who
believes ..." (Rom. 1:16). How can this verse encourage
you to be strong when you are tempted to be ashamed
or embarrassed to share your faith? What is the message
you have to share?

CHAPTER EIGHT

GOING PUBLIC

Ellie writes, "If we are going public with our faith, we will face the gates of hell. We will encounter resistance. We will catch flak." Have you ever suffered any kind of persecution for your faith? Have you ever encountered resistance when you've "held the line"? Explain.

Titus 3:3 says, "At one time, we too were foolish. We were disobedient. We were deceived. We were enslaved by all kinds of passions and pleasures." What kinds of behaviors and attitudes have you given up as a Christian?

Ellie tells the story of the pastor who challenged his congregation not to defend themselves for an entire week. If you were given the same challenge, how well do you think you would do? Are you willing to try it for a week?

What would your response be if someone said to you, "Christianity is a crutch for the weak"?

In the closing paragraph of this chapter, Ellie talks about the difficulties and challenges when you "take up the cross." What hardships have you encountered when you have taken up the cross? Ellie says, "When you take up the cross, you may even feel forsaken by God at times." Have you ever experienced this feeling? Explain.

CHAPTER NINE

THIRTY-ONE MILES

James 1:6 says, "He who doubts is like a wave of the sea, blown and tossed by the wind. That man should not think he will receive anything from the Lord; he is a double-minded man, unstable in all he does." Have you ever tossed and turned throughout the night, worrying about the same problem you prayed about before going to bed? Have you ever crossed your fingers, hoping God will "show up" in your situation? How can you confidently anticipate that He is at work, despite evidence to the contrary?

"One of the ways we need to affirm our sense of expectation is the way we approach God in prayer." Do you tend to pray in "broad strokes" or do you request specific answers? In the coming week, how can you concentrate on praying more specifically for something or someone?

Joshua and the priests had to stand in the river while thirty-one miles of water rushed by before it stopped. What are your "thirty-one miles"? What trouble is swirling around you? Do you have the faith to wait thirty-one miles to see the work of God unfold in His time? Describe a time when you believe that God began to work "as soon as" you asked for help even though you couldn't see help on the horizon at that time.

"I don't even know why I have to carry this. I don't see the good that can come out of it and I feel tired and burdened. But Lord ... if you want me to, I'll carry it." Do you ever feel this way? What burden are you carrying? What has stolen some of your hope and joy? What is pressing you up against the wall?

"Sometimes what we think is a disaster is a blessing in disguise." What disaster in your life has turned out to be a blessing? How did you see God work through the disaster?

CHAPTER TEN

WHAT DO THESE STONES MEAN?

Twelve men were commanded to each gather a large stone
from the middle of the now-dry Jordan River as a
reminder of God's faithfulness. Do you have any tangible
reminders of God's faithfulness to you? In what other
creative ways can you communicate God's faithfulness to
those around you?

If you were asked to explain the significance of communion
or baptism to a new Christian or a non-Christian, would
you know what to say? How about Easter? Christmas? Is
there anything special about your spiritual traditions of
those days that you could share?

Have family stories and histories been passed down to you?
Are they written down anywhere? If you have children
of your own, have you shared the stories with them?
How can you preserve your family histories for generations to come?

"We should have the sincere desire to help others and build them up in their faith." Who can you help? Who around you is struggling in a particular area that you might be able to build up?

This chapter includes the story of Charles Spurgeon explaining our need for the body (the Church), using a dying ember to illustrate a private pursuit of God. Have you ever been that "lone ember"? What was it like? What can we learn from Spurgeon's illustration?

In Luke 4:16, we read that Jesus "went to Nazareth, where he had been brought up, and on the Sabbath day he went into the synagogue, *as was his custom*." If Jesus, the Son of God, attended 'church' regularly, what should our view of regular worship be?

CHAPTER ELEVEN

A LEGACY WORTH LEAVING

What is the difference between a *legacy* and a *heritage*?
Which one can you influence? If your family story
doesn't seem particularly significant or worthy, what
encouragement do you have in terms of your legacy?

What will others remember about you? Do you think you
will be remembered for any particular accomplishments?
Will you be remembered for any particular character
traits?

Who has been significant in your life? What makes them
significant? Do you think you are significant in someone
else's life? How can you invest in the life of someone
else?

Are you pleased with how you are living "the dash"? If you could alter your dash, what changes would you make?

"If it's true that a person starts to look like his or her spouse after many years of marriage, imagine how that relates to Christians. We can 'aspire' to look more like Christ." What characteristics of Christ do you think people can see in you currently? What features of Christ would you like to acquire in time?

James 4:14 says, "Why, you do not even know what will happen tomorrow. What is your life? You are a mist that appears for a little while and then vanishes." What does this verse teach us about the importance of living each day for Christ and the urgency of sharing our faith to those around us?

CHAPTER TWELVE

PASSING ON WHAT MATTERS

Stone One: Pass on Encouragement

What people have been the biggest encouragers of your life?
Is there someone who believed in you even when you
might not have believed in yourself? Who can you
encourage in the days, weeks, and months to come? In
what way can you encourage that person?

Stone Two: Pass on an Awareness of Gifts and Capabilities

What special gifts and capabilities do you possess? What
special gifts or capabilities do you observe in those close
to you (children, spouse, friends, coworkers)? How can
you encourage and affirm them in those areas?

Stone Three: Pass on What You Value

What's important to you? What do you value above all else?
If your checkbook truly reveals what you value, what
would it indicate is important to you? How about your

calendar? Is there a discrepancy between what you *think* you value and how you spend your time and your money? Are there any changes you'd like to make in order to align these better?

Stone Four: Pass on a Priority on God's Word

What priority does God's Word have in your life? Are your family, coworkers, and friends able to see its value in your life? How can you strengthen your Christian witness to those around you?

Stone Five: Pass on Wisdom from Life's Experiences

Who has been there for you in times of trouble or uncertainty to encourage and comfort you with the words, "This too shall pass"? Can you think of situations where you have been comforted by the encouragement of someone who has shared a similar experience—and survived? Do you know of someone whom you can encourage because of the wisdom you have gained through similar life experiences (for example, divorce, miscarriage, aging parents, illness, etc.)?

NOTES

Chapter One: Capital "C" Christian

1 The Gallup Organization and the Center for Research on Religion & Urban Civil Society, "The Spiritual State of the Union" (March 8, 2003).

2 Francis Schaeffer, *He Is There and He Is Not Silent* (Wheaton, Ill.: Tyndale House Publishers, 1980).

3 Thomas Aquinas, *Summa Theologica* (Ephesians), complete English Translation from Latin edition, (Allen, Tex.: Thomas More Publishing, 1981).

4 Ibid.

Chapter Three: Destined for More

5 Max Lucado, *Just Like Jesus* (Nashville, Tenn.: Thomas Nelson, Inc., 1998).

Chapter Six: Leaving the Sands of Uncertainty

6 C. S. Lewis, *Mere Christianity* (New York: HarperSanFrancisco, 2001).

Chapter Seven: What Now?

7 Amy Carmichael, "Calvary Love," from *If*, by Dohnavur Fellowship, Fort Washington, Penn.: Christian Literature Crusade.

Chapter Nine: What Do These Stones Mean?

8 The song was written in 1832 by Edward Mote, and the tune in 1863 by William B. Bradbury.

9 Kathy Troccoli, "Break My Heart," from *Love Has A Name* (Sony/ATV Tunes LLC, 2000).

Chapter Twelve: Passing On What Matters

10 Author unknown

A New York stoop!

The "Be" series by Cook author Dr. Warren Wiersbe
has been integral to Ellie's teaching

THE LOFARO FAMILY IN D.C.

FRESH CANNOLIS

ELLIE AND KATHY TROCCOLI
IN NEW YORK

Two heroes of the faith
Chuck Colson and Dr. James Dobson

A mother and child reunion

The Word at Work . . .

What would you do if you wanted to share God's love with children on the streets of your city? That's the dilemma David C. Cook faced in 1870s Chicago. His answer was to create literature that would capture children's hearts.

Out of those humble beginnings grew a worldwide ministry that has used literature to proclaim God's love and disciple generation after generation. Cook Communications Ministries is committed to personal discipleship—to helping people of all ages learn God's Word, embrace his salvation, walk in his ways, and minister in his name.

Opportunities—and Crisis

We live in a land of plenty—including plenty of Christian literature! But what about the rest of the world? Jesus commanded, "Go and make disciples of all nations" (Matt. 28:19) and we want to obey this commandment. But how does a publishing organization "go" into all the world?

There are five times as many Christians around the world as there are in North America. Christian workers in many of these countries have no more than a New Testament, or perhaps a single shared copy of the Bible, from which to learn and teach.

We are committed to sharing what God has given us with such Christians.

A vital part of Cook Communications Ministries is our international outreach, Cook Communications Ministries International (CCMI). Your purchase of this book, and of other books and Christian-growth products from Cook, enables CCMI to provide Bibles and Christian literature to people in more than 150 languages in 65 countries.

Cook Communications Ministries is a not-for-profit, self-supporting organization. Revenues from sales of our books, Bible curriculum, and other church and home products not only fund our U.S. ministry, but also fund our CCMI ministry around the world. One hundred percent of donations to CCMI go to our international literature programs.

... Around the World

CCMI reaches out internationally in three ways:

· Our premier International Christian Publishing Institute (ICPI) trains leaders from nationally led publishing houses around the world to develop evangelism and discipleship materials to transform lives in their countries.

· We provide literature for pastors, evangelists, and Christian workers in their national language. We provide study helps for pastors and lay leaders in many parts of the world, such as China, India, Cuba, Iran, and Vietnam.

· We reach people at risk—refugees, AIDS victims, street children, and famine victims—with God's Word. CCMI puts literature that shares the Good News into the hands of people at spiritual risk—people who might die before they hear the name of Jesus and are transformed by his love.

Word Power—God's Power

Faith Kidz, RiverOak, Honor, Life Journey, Victor, NexGen — every time you purchase a book produced by Cook Communications Ministries, you not only meet a vital personal need in your life or in the life of someone you love, but you're also a part of ministering to José in Colombia, Humberto in Chile, Gousa in India, or Lidiane in Brazil. You help make it possible for a pastor in China, a child in Peru, or a mother in West Africa to enjoy a life-changing book. And because you helped, children and adults around the world are learning God's Word and walking in his ways.

Thank you for your partnership in helping to disciple the world. May God bless you with the power of his Word in your life.

For more information about our international ministries, visit www.ccmi.org.